I0426786

The American Ali Baba & His 40 Thieves

A modern tragedy rooted in an ancient Arabic tale

by

Professor Alex Shami

authorHOUSE™

1663 LIBERTY DRIVE, SUITE 200
BLOOMINGTON, INDIANA 47403
(800) 839-8640
WWW.AUTHORHOUSE.COM

© 2004 Professor Alex Shami
All Rights Reserved.

No part of this book may be reproduced, stored in a retrieval system, or transmitted by any means without the written permission of the author.

First published by AuthorHouse 08/27/04

ISBN: 1-4184-8670-1 (sc)
ISBN: 1-4184-8671-X (dj)

Library of Congress Control Number: 2004095769

Printed in the United States of America
Bloomington, Indiana

This book is printed on acid-free paper.

Disclaimer
An extraordinary number of sources provided the material for this book, far too numerous to list. For a source of any information or quote, please contact the author.

Author's Note

The author sincerely hopes that the information presented in this book will give the reader pause. Consider the direction in which this country heads. Consider life without rights that protect us. Consider a land raped of its precious trees, protected spaces and wonderful wildlife. Consider a life of slavery, for the longer we remain on the current track, the more likely this country will become a land of controlled have-nots ruled by the wealthy mighty. The signs are rapidly pointing in that direction.

The people of this nation possess the power to change that direction. To that end, we should heed the powerful words in our Declaration of Independence:

Whenever any Form of Government becomes destructive of these ends, it is the Right of the People to alter or to abolish it, and to institute new Government, laying its foundation on such principles and organizing its powers in such form, as to them shall seem most likely to effect their Safety and Happiness.

Table of Contents

Introduction

The inspiration for this book lies in one tale within the Arabian Nights, a collection of imaginative folk stories told in ancient Persia and throughout the Arab World and written first in Arabic. One such yarn, "Ali Baba and the Forty Thieves", seems to apply to the story unfolding in the current presidential administration in Washington. Is it a tragedy? Yes, indeed, for no administration in memory established its foundation on more greed, lies or self-serving agendas than the Bush Administration. It is a tragedy perpetrated by the rich and powerful to conquer and enforce their New World Order.

"Ali Baba" is a tale of theft, greed, secrecy, deception and murder, all ingredients found in the tragedy unfolding in Washington. Bush administrators have shredded the Bill of Rights upon which this great nation was founded, rolled back laws that protected the environment, thrown the American school system into disarray, and fattened the rich man's wallet. Additionally, the Bush Administration plotted, schemed, and carried out a pre-emptive war against Iraq based on lies and launched arrogantly in the face of worldwide opposition.

The most recent turn of events - revelation of Iraqi prisoner abuse by US military personnel - revealed more secrets and more lies, generating global outrage. Each day, the Bush Administration's waters grow murkier.

This book contains nine sections, as follows:

Section 1. The Ancient Tale of "Ali Baba and the Forty Thieves" appears here in streamlined English. It is an easy-to-read summary of one of the most popular tales from the Arabian Nights. For those readers who are unfamiliar with this ancient magical collection of stories, we hope you will appreciate this shortened version.

Section 2. Early American Perspectives. This section presents the vision of America's forefathers for the government they formed. Also included here is a copy of the Bill of Rights, which these early American visionaries added to the US Constitution to assure all citizens the kind of protection they need in a variety of situations. It is imperative that all Americans understand the Bill of Rights, for the Bush Administration - through the Patriot Act and other measures - has eroded those rights. Rights lost are difficult to regain. Americans must protect and defend these rights set forth more than 200 years ago by our forefathers.

Section 3. Dark Influences in American Foreign Policy. In this section, four individuals stand out as those who, over time, have steered American foreign policy into a direction that prioritizes war over peace, greed over concern, and that has won more enemies than friends around the world. Those men are Henry Kissinger, known in some circles as the Ariel Sharon of America, Prince Bandar, the Saudi ambassador to Washington, Ariel Sharon, and Zbigniew Brzezinski, whose plan for world domination became one of the bibles of the Bush II Administration. These men have cast dark shadows on our government that have not only damaged the US overseas but also cost the American people precious lives and countless fortunes.

Section 4. The Bush Dynasty. This section examines the American family that more closely resembles a dynasty than any other family has. First, we look at a great grandfather and two grandfathers, who participated in any number of nefarious deeds to satisfy their greedy agendas. Then, we examine three sons, who picked up the scepter and built lucrative careers based on lies, deception and greed. They spared no criminal activity in the process. Three grandsons followed - Neil, Jeb and George W, who carved out their own niches in the wall of greed established as the basis of life by their predecessors.

Section 5. The American Ali Baba - George W. Bush. Just as the threads of greed, lies and deception weave their way through the ancient tale of Ali Baba, so do they tie up corruption into a tidy package in the Bush II Administration. The rich get richer. The poor become more enslaved. For a man who admits to not being intellectual - and, by all appearances, is not intelligent - George W is the puppet of the neocons that surround him and manipulate government entities to secure whatever they need to further their agendas. A puppet with a permanent smirk, Bush is at the mercy of the puppet masters, obeying orders about what to say, what not to say, and how to avoid saying any more than necessary.

Section 6. His 40 Thieves. This section could feature far more than 40 thieves, those individuals who methodically erode the rights of all Americans and tarnish world opinion of this great nation. In the course of research for this section, it was startling to discover the pervasiveness of hawkish Israeli/ Likud influence in the Bush Administration. Of the 40 thieves examined in this section, most have serious - if not primary - allegiance to Israel. That opens the question, just who is running this country, anyway? If suddenly, a large number of Japanese, Italian or Brazilian individuals called the shots about US domestic and foreign policies from the inner sanctum of American government, might we be concerned? Why, then, are we not concerned about the inordinately high number of pro-Israeli officials in our federal government? As former US Senator William Fulbright said many years ago, "Israel controls the United States Senate." Today, it also controls Congress, the US Senate, the White House, the Pentagon…

Section 7. <u>Runners-up.</u> There are many more than 40 individuals in the Bush II Administration, as well as those in external advisory positions, who have contributed to the theft of America's good will, resources and people. We list and briefly describe some of their qualifications for thievery here.

Section 8. <u>Thieves of Truth: The Mainstream Media.</u> Just as the "first tragedy of war is truth" so it is true in all areas of our lives where the mainstream media rob us of our right to know the truth. The secrecy imposed by the Bush II Administration enveloped the mainstream media. Consequently, the White House has controlled the media to report not what Americans want to know but what the government thinks we should know. Does anything about this ring a bell? Check this section and see.

Section 9. <u>Points of Light Awards.</u> One section must give hope to the reader. This section does that. Awards go to those people who, with the courage of their convictions, set examples for all Americans to return this country to a nation of truth, honor, justice and freedom.

ALI BABA AND THE FORTY THIEVES

The Ancient Arabic Tale — Abbreviated

A long, long time ago, in ancient Baghdad, there lived two brothers, Kasim and Ali Baba. They divided equally their inheritance and soon squandered it. Kasim married the daughter of a rich merchant. When he died, Kasim became the owner of a large shop filled with costly merchandise, as well as much gold. The townspeople knew him as a wealthy man.

In contrast, Ali Baba married a poor woman. They lived in a hovel, and he eked out a meager living selling dry fuel that he gathered in the nearby forest and carried on his three mules to the bazaar.

One day, Ali Baba gathered the dry fuel that he needed and started to leave the forest. Suddenly he saw many horsemen. He feared they might be bandits who would kill him and drive off his donkeys. He ran, but the horsemen were so close that Ali Baba knew he could not escape.

He hid his mules under some bushes and climbed high up in a huge tree. There, he could watch below but no one could see him.

The horsemen — 40 in all — approached a huge rock and dismounted. Ali Baba studied them closely and figured they were highwaymen who had robbed a caravan and brought their booty to stash safely.

They rested under the tree, unbridled their horses and removed their saddlebags. The captain pressed forward until he found a certain place in the rock. There, he spoke two strange words, "Open, Sesame!" At once, a wide door opened. The robbers entered, and the door closed behind them.

While the robbers were inside the cave, Ali Baba remained in the tree. Just as he thought about jumping onto one of the horses and riding off, the cave door opened. The captain left first, counting all the men as they left. He then closed the door with the magic words, "Shut, Sesame!"

The robbers bridled their horses and off they all rode in the same direction they came. Ali Baba watched their departure from the tree.

He tried the magic words. "Open, Sesame!" No sooner had he spoken than the door opened. The cave was very large with high vaulted ceilings.

He expected to find only a gloomy robber's den, but to his surprise, he saw a huge room filled with stacks of silks and brocades and mounds upon mounds of colorful carpets. He also found an immeasurable amount of gold and silver coins. He realized then that generations of thieves must have used the cave to store their loot.

Ali Baba decided to take only bags of gold, which he hid under the dry fuel on his mules. Casual observers would think he was carrying his usual load from the forest. He then pronounced the magic words, "Shut, Sesame!" to close the door.

When he reached home, he drove the mules into the courtyard and closed the outer gate. He unloaded the sticks and dry fuel, and then removed the bags of gold, which he took to his wife.

As soon as his wife saw the bags of coins, she accused Ali Baba of stealing. "I am no robber," he said. "You should rejoice at our good fortune." He then told her of his adventure and began to heap the gold onto the table before her. It dazzled her eyes, and her heart delighted at her husband's discovery.

She started to count the gold, but Ali Baba interrupted her. "Silly woman, how long will it take you to count all those coins?"

His wife replied, "You are right! I would still like to know how much we have." He agreed but cautioned her to speak to no one.

She went to Kasim's home to borrow a scale. Her sister-in-law was suspicious, knowing how poor Ali Baba was, so she secretly smeared wax over the inside of the weight pan, hoping some of whatever Ali Baba's wife weighed would stick to the wax.

Ali Baba's wife, suspecting nothing, took the scales home and weighed the coins, while her husband dug a hole to bury the treasure. Later, the wife returned the scales, not realizing that a coin had stuck to the wax.

When Kasim's wife saw the gold coin, she became furious, wondering how such a poor man received so much gold that he needed to weigh it. When Kasim returned home, she said to him, "You consider yourself wealthy, but your brother is far richer than you. He has so much gold that he needs scales to weigh it, while you are satisfied to count yours."

Kasim's wife told Kasim how she used the wax to discover why Ali Baba needed the scales. She showed him a gold coin, which bore the inscription of an ancient king.

Kasim's jealousy kept him awake that night. Next morning, he went to Ali Baba. "My brother, everyone thinks you are poor, but I understand you have so much wealth, you needed scales to weigh it."

Ali Baba replied, "What are you talking about?"

Then, Kasim showed him the gold coin that was stuck in the wax. "Don't pretend you do not know. You have thousands of coins, and my wife found this one when your wife returned the scales."

Ali Baba felt it would cause only ill will and hard feelings to keep the matter hidden. He told Kasim about the bandits and the stored treasure.

"Tell me where the cave is and the magic words to open and close the door," Kasim insisted. "If you do not tell me, I will notify the authorities and you will lose your new treasure and go to jail."

Ali Baba told Kasim everything, including the magic words. The next day, Kasim took 10 mules into the forest and found the cave that Ali Baba described. He stood at the door. "Open, Sesame!" The door opened wide, and Kasim entered, as the door closed behind him. Inside, he saw jewels and treasures everywhere, and gathered up bags of gold.

As fate had it, Kasim forgot the magic words. "Open, Barley!" The door did not budge. He named all the grains he knew, except sesame. He became so upset that he forgot about the mules and the bags of gold. He paced back and forth in the cave, trying to remember the words.

By noon, the robbers returned to the cave and saw mules wandering near the entrance. They wondered what brought them to the cave. The captain spoke the magic words.

Inside the cave, Kasim had heard the sound of approaching horses. He fell to the ground, fearing that the bandits returned and would surely kill him. As the door opened, Kasim rushed out hoping to make good an escape. He ran right into the captain, who knocked him to the ground. A robber drew his sword and cut Kasim in two.

The robbers returned the bags Kasim had heaped by the door. In all the excitement, however, they did not notice any of the missing gold that Ali Baba took. They were more concerned that someone had entered the cave. They knew that no man could drop down through the skylights and no man could enter the door unless he knew the magic words.

They quartered Kasim's body and hung the parts on either side of the door inside the cave. They left, closed the door and rode off into the forest.

When night fell and Kasim did not return home, his wife became uneasy. She ran to Ali Baba, "Kasim has not returned. You know where he went. I am afraid something terrible happened to him."

Ali Baba tried to comfort her. "Kasim chose a roundabout way to avoid the town. He will be here soon."

Kasim's wife, feeling comforted, returned home. Halfway through the night, when he had still not returned, she worried. She dared not cry aloud, for fear the neighbors would hear her, come to her house, and learn the secret. "Why did I share the secret with him and show jealousy of Ali Baba? It is my fault that disaster has come down upon me."

Early the next morning, she rushed to Ali Baba's house and begged him to look for his brother. He took his mules to the forest. When he reached the rock that housed the cave of treasures, he noticed freshly spilled blood, but he did not find his brother or his mules.

"Open, Sesame!" he said and rushed into the cave. There, he saw Kasim's dead body. He was frightened beyond words. He wrapped his brother's body and laid it on one of his mules, covering it carefully with sticks.

Ali Baba then placed more bags of gold on the other mules and covered them as well. When he returned home, he gave the mules with gold to his wife and urged her to bury it. He took the mule with the corpse to his widow's house. He knocked gently on the door.

Kasim had a very smart slave girl named Morgiana. She admitted Ali Baba and the mule into the courtyard. When he unloaded the body, he said, "Oh, Morgiana, hurry and prepare for the burial of your master."

At that instant, Kasim's widow, seeing Ali Baba, cried, "Oh, brother, what news do you bring? You look sad. Tell me quickly what happened." He told her everything, but cautioned her, "What was to happen happened. We must keep this matter a secret, for our lives depend on it."

She wept and wept. "Telling the secret to my husband brought this terrible fate. Now, for your safety, I promise never to tell anyone again."

Ali Baba responded, "Nothing can change what has happened. Be patient until your days of mourning end. Then, I will make you my wife and you will live a life of comfort and happiness. Do not let my first wife anger you or show signs of jealousy, for she is a kind, tender-hearted woman." The widow, crying loudly, said, "Whatever you wish."

Then Ali Baba left her weeping and returned to Morgiana. They discussed Kasim's burial arrangements. After a while, he returned home with his mule.

As soon as Ali Baba left, Morgiana ran to the pharmacy. To protect what had happened, she asked for medication for a man with distemper. The pharmacist asked, "Who in your house needs this medicine?"

Morgiana replied, "My master is sick almost to death. For many days, he has not spoken or eaten, and we are worried he might not live."

The next day, she requested more medicine. She took the potion and sighed aloud, deceptively, "I fear he will be dead before I return home."

Early on the second day, Morgiana veiled herself and went to an old tailor, Baba Mustafa, who made burial cloths. As soon as he opened his shop, she handed him a gold piece and said, "Blindfold your eyes and come with me." Mustafa protested, so Morgiana gave him another coin. He agreed. She tied a cloth over his eyes and led him to Kasim's house.

There, in a darkened room, she removed the blindfold and told him to sew her master's body together. She gave him a cloth, told him to make a shroud for Kasim's body, and promised him another gold coin. The tailor did as instructed, and Morgiana paid him. Then, she took him to his shop, and returned home.

After Morgiana and Ali Baba prepared the body for burial, she went to the mosque and asked the imam to come and read the prayers for the dead. At the house, four neighbors carried the coffin to where the imam delivered prayers. After the prayer reading, four other men carried the coffin to the cemetery. Morgiana walked ahead of them. She wore no veil over her head, and she wept loudly, while Ali Baba and other neighbors followed.

They buried Kasim. Then, the women all gathered at the widow's house and consoled her.

Ali Baba stayed home for the 40 days to mourn the loss of his brother. At the end of that time, he married the widow and moved his household into Kasim's house. Then he appointed Kasim's eldest son to carry on his father's business.

One day, the robbers checked the cave and were surprised to see no sign of the slain body. They also noticed that much of the gold had disappeared. The captain said, "We must look into this matter, so that we do not suffer such a great loss."

To find out who it was, they decided that one of the robbers should dress as a foreign merchant, go to the town and search for any clues that would lead them to the suspect. Hereat said, "I will find the answer or die trying."

Very early the next morning, he went to the bazaar. Only one shop was open — that of the tailor, Baba Mustafa, who was busy sewing.

"Good day," greeted Hereat. "It is still dark. How can you see to sew?" The tailor replied, "You are a stranger here. Despite my age, my eyesight is so sharp that yesterday I sewed up a dead body while sitting in a darkened room."

The bandit knew he had found a link to the man he sought, but he pressed further. "Surely you jest. You mean that you stitched a burial cloth for a corpse, for that is your business." The tailor answered, "It does not concern you. Do not ask any questions."

Hereat placed a gold coin in the tailor's hand and continued, "I do not want to discover all your secrets. I only want to know one thing. Where did you do that job? Can you take me there?"

The tailor explained how a woman blindfolded him and led him to the house and back to his shop. He said he could not direct him there.

The bandit replied, "I will blindfold you and lead you as the woman did." He slipped another coin into the tailor's hand and repeated the blindfolded walk. Baba Mustafa counted his steps, then stopped suddenly. "This is how far I came with her."

They stopped in front of Kasim's house, where now lived his brother Ali Baba. The bandit made white chalk marks on the door to help him find it again. He removed the blindfold. "Thank you for this favor." He left and the bandit returned to the forest.

Not long after, Morgiana left the house. She noticed the white chalk marks on the door and figured some enemy had made the sign so that he might return and bring trouble to her master. She proceeded to make similar chalk marks on all of her neighbors' doors and kept the matter secret.

Meanwhile, Hereat told his comrades how he found the clue. The captain and thieves went to the city by different routes. Hereat led the captain straight to the house and said, "Here is the house of the man we seek." However, the captain saw that all the dwellings had similar chalk marks. "How do you know which house is the one you marked?"

Hereat was confused. "I did put a sign on a door, but I do not know how these other signs came to be. I cannot say for sure which door I marked." The captain returned to the bazaar and said to his men, "We cannot find the house that our comrade marked. Return to the forest. I will soon follow."

Later, in the cave, the captain imprisoned Hereat for leading them through the city to no end. "I will show special favor to whoever tells me where to find the one who stole our property."

Another bandit stepped forward. "I am ready to go and investigate this case." The captain gave him many promises and then dispatched him.

By some stroke of fate, the bandit went first to the house of Baba Mustafa. He persuaded him with gifts of gold to repeat what he had done for Hereat. When they arrived at Ali Baba's door, the bandit marked the door with red chalk to distinguish it from the others in the neighborhood. He then returned to the cave.

Morgiana happened upon the red chalk marks and proceeded to mark all the other doors in similar fashion, telling no one of her deed.

Back at the cave, the bandit proudly said, "Captain, I marked the right house with red chalk." The bandits again went to town and saw every house marked with red chalk. The captain, exceedingly displeased, put the second bandit into jail. 'Two men failed to find this house. Only I can find it,' he mused.

The captain went to town and found Baba Mustafa, who earned more gold for leading him to Ali Baba's house. He made no outward sign, but impressed in his mind the image of the house.

Returning to the forest, he said, "I know the house and will have no trouble finding it again. Buy 19 mules, 1 large jar of mustard oil, and 37 large leather vessels. Excluding the two in jail and me, there are 37 of you. Two by two, I will arm you and put you in jars on the mules. The nineteenth mule will carry a man in a jar on one side and a jar full of oil. I will disguise myself as an oil merchant, driving the mules into town. At night, we will arrive at the house and ask permission of its master to wait there until morning. After this, we will find an excuse in the dark hours to rise early, find him and slay him."

This plan pleased the bandits, who immediately purchased the mules, huge leather jars, and the oil. Three days later, shortly before dusk, each man hid in one of the jars. The captain disguised himself and went to town, reaching Ali Baba's house by dusk.

Ali Baba was taking an evening stroll. The captain saluted him, "I come from a far village with oil, but I arrived too late. I do not know where to spend the night. Would you let me stay here and let the mules rest and eat?"

Ali Baba remembered having heard the man's voice but did not identify it as the captain's, because he wore a disguise. He welcomed him and told him to enjoy his home. He showed him an empty shed where he could tie his mules and ordered a slave boy to feed and water them. He ordered Morgiana to feed him and prepare a guest bed for him.

He also told her, "Early tomorrow I will go to the bathhouse. Give my slave boy Abdullah a suit of clean white clothes for me to wear when I return, and prepare some broth overnight that I can drink then."

Ali Baba retired for the night. After eating his supper, the captain went to the shed and checked on his mules. In complete privacy, he spoke to his men in the jars, "Tonight at midnight, when you hear my voice, quickly use your sharp knives to open the leather jars and come without delay."

Passing through the kitchen, he found the bed that Morgiana had prepared for him. "If you need anything else, please ask," she said.

Meanwhile, Morgiana did as her master had instructed. She took clean white clothes to Abdullah. Then she began boiling the broth. She blew the dwindling flames to make the fire burn more briskly.

After a short while, she checked the broth, but found that the oil lamps had gone out. There was no more oil and she could not see. "Why are you making such a fuss?" quizzed Abdullah. "There is plenty of oil in the shed. Take some."

Morgiana thanked him for his suggestion, and went to the shed where all the leather jars stood neatly in rows. As she approached one of the jars, the thief inside thought the footsteps belonged to his captain. He whispered, 'Is it time for us to come out?'

Morgiana was startled at the sound of a human voice, but as a witty woman, she replied, "The time is not yet come." Then she said to herself, 'I think I have uncovered a treacherous plot against my master.'

She went from jar to jar, and each time a thief asked if it was time, she responded in a voice like the oil merchant's, "The time is not yet come." After passing all the jars, she thought, 'Lord, my master took this man in believing him to be an oil merchant, but instead he brought thieves to rob and kill him.'

As Morgiana reached the last jar, she found it full of oil. She returned to the kitchen and lit the lamps. She then took a large pot and set it on the fire. She filled it with oil, piled wood on the hearth and built a huge fire.

She then poured the hot oil into the leather jars, scalding the thieves to death. Using her good sense, the slave girl had saved the household from disaster, all done quietly and secretly. After she was satisfied that all the thieves were dead, she returned to the kitchen and brewed Ali Baba's broth.

Less than an hour later, the captain awoke from his sleep and saw that the night was dark and silent. He clapped his hands and called aloud three times as a signal to his men to come out, but he did not hear a sound in return. He went to the shed, believing his bandits had fallen asleep.

Approaching the nearest jar, he smelled oil and burned flesh. When he touched the jar, it was hot. He found the other jars in the same condition. He knew that fate had befallen his thieves and feared for his own safety. He climbed the wall, dropped into a garden and made his escape.

Morgiana waited to see the captain return from the shed, but when he did not come, she knew he had escaped. With the captain gone and the thieves dead, she laid down to sleep in perfect peace.

Although two hours of darkness remained, Ali Baba awoke and went to the bathhouse, not knowing a thing of what happened earlier.

The sun rose over the horizon when Ali Baba emerged from the baths, and was surprised to see the jars still standing in the shed. "Why has the oil merchant not taken his oil and mules to market yet?" Morgiana answered, "I will tell you. Look in this jar and see if there is oil inside."

Ali Baba opened the jar and what he saw frightened him. Morgiana said, "Fear not. He is dead." Hearing her words of comfort, Ali Baba asked, "What evils have we escaped? By what means did fate meet these men?"

Morgiana explained what happened and how she killed the thieves, one by one. Ali Baba checked all the jars and found in each an armed man, dead. He soon recovered from shock and asked about the oil merchant.

"That villain was no merchant," she said, "but a treacherous assassin. I will tell you more, but first, you should drink some broth for your health." So, Ali Baba went into the house and Morgiana served her master. She then related the entire adventure to Ali Baba. "For days, I had an idea something was brewing, but I did not tell you for fear the neighbors would discover our secret. Now, I have no choice."

Upon hearing the story, Ali Baba rejoiced, "I am very pleased with what you did. What can I do for you? I will never forget your brave deeds."

He and Abdullah buried the corpses in the garden and hid the leather jars and the weapons they took from the bandits. Ali Baba sent the mules to the bazaar and sold them.

Ali Baba remained uneasy, however, aware that the captain and two robbers could come any time. He stayed at home and did not speak of any of the recent events.

Meanwhile, the captain fled to the forest. He resolved that he must kill him and decided he must do the deed alone. After he disposed of Ali Baba, he would form another band of thieves.

The next morning, he rose and dressed in suitable city attire. 'Surely the murder of so many men reached the ears of the authorities and they brought Ali Baba to justice, leveled his house and confiscated all his belongings. Someone surely heard about all this.'

He asked people in town, "What strange things have happened during the past few days?" They told him many things but did not mention Ali Baba. The captain realized that Ali Baba was a clever man. He took all the gold and killed many men, yet no one knew about his deeds. The captain realized he must watch his step or fall victim himself.

He hired a shop in the bazaar, where he sold the finest wares from his forest treasure house. By chance, his shop faced that of the deceased Kasim, where his son, Ali Baba's nephew, now traded. The captain, who gave himself the name Khwajah Hasan, met him and other shopkeepers. He was especially cordial to the nephew, who was handsome and well dressed.

A few days later, Ali Baba stopped to see his nephew. The captain immediately recognized him. After that, he showed even more favor to the nephew, to deceive him. He gave him gifts and fed him the finest foods.

In time, Ali Baba's nephew thought it was only proper to invite the merchant to dinner. He sought his uncle's advice. Ali Baba said, "It is good for you should treat your friend in the best way. Tomorrow take Khwajah Hasan on a walk to enjoy the fresh air. Bring him here. I will take care of everything."

Accordingly, the nephew took Khwajah Hasan on a walk and as they returned, he led him by his uncle's house. The young man knocked on the door. "My uncle has heard much of your goodness toward me. He would like very much to meet you."

Khwajah Hasan rejoiced at the prospect of gaining access to his enemy's house, but he hesitated. He made excuses and started to walk away.

When Abdullah opened the door, the nephew persuaded him to enter. Khwajah Hasan entered with a great show of cheerfulness. Ali Baba welcomed him, "I am most grateful to you for showing such favor to my nephew."

Khwajah Hasan said, "Your nephew took my fancy, and I am very pleased with him, for although he is young, he has much wisdom."

They continued their friendly conversation. Soon, the guest rose to depart. "I must leave now, but one day I will come again." Ali Baba would not let him leave. "Where are you going, my friend? I invite you to dine with me. Then you can go home in peace."

Khwajah Hasan replied, "I am grateful for your invitation, but I must excuse myself. I cannot stay longer."

"Tell me what is so urgent?" asked Ali Baba.

"My physician orders me not eat any food prepared with salt," he said.

"Do not go. I will forbid my cook to not use any salt." He went to the kitchen and told Morgiana. She agreed to comply, but wondered who would make such an order. She wanted to look at him.

When all the meat and other dishes were ready, she and Abdullah set the table. No sooner did she see Khwajah Hasan than she knew who he was, even

9

in his clever disguise. She noticed a dagger under his robe. 'So!' she said to herself, 'this man wants only to slay my master. I must stop him!'

When the men finished eating, Morgiana set out fresh and dried fruit and a flask of wine. She then went to another room with Abdullah, pretending to eat her supper.

When Khwajah Hasan realized the way was clear, he thought, 'It is time. I will kill Ali Baba and escape through the garden. If his nephew moves one finger, I will stab him, too. First, I must wait until the slaves eat their meal and lie down to rest.'

Morgiana watched him. 'I must not allow this villain to harm my master,' she said to herself. So, she dressed as an exotic dancer and veiled her face. She tied a belt of gold and silver around her waist, where she tucked a bejeweled dagger. Then she said to Abdullah, "Bring your tambourine, so we can entertain for our master's guest."

They presented themselves and asked permission. Ali Baba said, "Dance now and do your best to make our guest enjoy himself." Khwajah Hasan added, "You do indeed provide much pleasant entertainment!"

As Morgiana danced, she suddenly brandished the dagger and paced exotically, making a spectacle that pleased them most of all. Then, she took the tambourine and, as was the custom, solicited tips from the merrymakers.

First, she stood before Ali Baba, who threw a gold coin into the tambourine, and then his nephew, who did likewise. Then Khwajah Hasan pulled out his purse. Morgiana, brave and quick, plunged the dagger into his heart and the guest fell dead.

Ali Baba cried out in anger, "What have you done?" She replied, "He was your deadly enemy. Look at him. He was the oil merchant with the band of robbers. He came only to kill you."

Ali Baba lavished her with gratitude. "Twice now you have saved my life from this man. You are now free. As a reward, I wed you to my nephew." Turning to the young man, he said, "Marry Morgiana, who is a model of duty and loyalty."

The nephew consented to the marriage. The three then buried the body in the garden. For many years, no one knew what happened there. Time smiled upon Ali Baba and a new source of wealth opened to him.

For fear of the two remaining thieves, Ali Baba never visited the forest cave since the day he removed his brother's corpse. However, one morning, he went there and, cautiously, finding no signs of man or horse, approached the cave door. "Open, Sesame!" Inside, he saw hoards of gold and silver. He felt reassured that none of the thieves remained alive, and no one else knew the secret to entering the cave. He loaded gold and silver onto his horse.

In the days that followed, he showed the treasure to his sons and his grandsons and taught them how to use magic words to open and close the cave door. Thus, Ali Baba and his household lived all their lives in wealth and happiness.

Early American Perspectives

An elective despotism was not the government we fought for.
Thomas Jefferson

In 1689, John Locke, an English philosopher, wrote his "Second Treatise on Civil Government" to justify the English Revolution of the year before, to reject the idea of the "Divine Right of Kings", and to dispute St. Thomas Aquinas' view of the origin of the state.

Locke's ideas, in concert with many other contributions from thinkers and religions throughout history, were the basis for the philosophical justification for the American Revolution and his concept of the rights of man are basic to the United States Constitution.

According to Locke's "Social Contract" theory, the only reason the government exists is to preserve the life, liberty and property of the citizens and it has no power except that which is used for the good of the people. The basic rights of the people, therefore, limit the power of the ruler, who has no right, divine or otherwise, to interfere with them.

Locke concluded that if the government breaks the trust of the people who establish it or if it interferes with the liberty of the citizens, they have a right to rebel and make a new contract under which they may govern themselves more conveniently. This right to rebel was the theory behind the U.S. Declaration of Independence, which declared that the colonies found the government under the King of England to be highly inconvenient as well as detrimental to their liberties.

America's history as an independent nation began on July 4, 1776, when representatives of the 13 colonies signed the Declaration of Independence. At this point, although we had declared ourselves free of English rule, there was no system of national government, so a Second Continental Congress assembled to form one.

Within the Declaration of Independence, the authors included a statement of critical importance then and now — the right to overthrow a corrupt government, just as the colonists overthrew a corrupt King George III of England:

> *We hold these truths to be self-evident, that all men are created equal, among these are Life, Liberty and the pursuit of Happiness — That to secure these rights, Governments are instituted among Men, deriving their just powers from the consent of the governed — That whenever any Form of Government becomes destructive of these ends, it is the Right of the People to alter or to abolish it, and to institute new Government, laying*

its foundation on such principles and organizing its powers in such form, as to them shall seem most likely to effect their Safety and Happiness. Prudence, indeed, will dictate that Governments long established should not be changed for light and transient causes; and accordingly all experience hath shewn, that mankind are more disposed to suffer, while evils are sufferable, than to right themselves by abolishing the forms to which they are accustomed. But when a long train of abuses and usurpations, pursuing invariably the same Object evinces a design to reduce them under absolute Despotism, it is their right, it is their duty, to throw off such Government, and to provide new Guards for their future security.

During the debates on the adoption of the Constitution, its opponents repeatedly charged that the Constitution, as initially drafted, would open the way to tyranny by the central government.

Fresh in their minds was the memory of the British violation of civil rights before and during the American Revolution. They demanded a "bill of rights" that would spell out the immunities of individual citizens.

A Philadelphia newspaper assailed the sweeping power of the central government, the usurpation of State Sovereignty, and the absence a bill of rights guaranteeing individual liberties such as freedom of speech and freedom of religion. "The United States are to be melted down, into a despotic empire, dominated by well born aristocrats."

This echoed a fear that the new government would become one controlled by the wealthy, established families and the culturally refined. The common working people were in danger of subjugation to the will of an all-powerful authority — remote and inaccessible to the people. Such an authority, Americans had fought a war against only a few years earlier.

Articles 3 to 12, once ratified by three-fourths of the State Legislatures, constitute the first 10 Amendments, which we know as the Bill of Rights. They guaranteed everyone, rich and poor, rights that the English denied them.

When James Madison, a serious student of history, drafted these amendments to the Constitution, he drew heavily upon the ideas put forth in the Virginia Declaration of Rights, written by George Mason.

Selected quotes from the early American leaders:

Benjamin Franklin: "They that can give up essential liberty to obtain a little temporary safety deserve neither liberty nor safety."

Benjamin Franklin: (As told to a French correspondent in 1788): "The formation of the new government had been like a game of dice, with many players of diverse prejudices and interests unable to make uncontested moves."

George Washington (in his farewell address as the first President of the United States, 1796): "So, likewise, a passionate attachment of one nation for another produces a variety of evils. Sympathy for the favorite nation, facilitating the illusion of an imaginary common interest in cases where no real common interest exists, and infusing into one the enmities of the other, betrays the former into a participation in the quarrels and wars of the latter without adequate inducement or justification."

James Madison (in a letter to Thomas Jefferson): 'The welding of these clashing interests was a task more difficult than can be well conceived by those who were not concerned in the execution of it." Late in his life, Madison would declare: "No government can be perfect, and that which is the least imperfect is therefore the best government."

Thomas Jefferson (1802): "Though written constitutions may be violated in moments of passion or delusion, yet they furnish a text to which those who are watchful may again rally and recall the people. They fix, too, for the people the principles of their political creed."

Thomas Jefferson (1809): "Aware of the tendency of power to degenerate into abuse, the worthies of our country have secured its independence by the establishment of a Constitution and form of government for our nation, calculated to prevent as well as to correct abuse."

Thomas Jefferson (1816): "[To establish republican government, it is necessary to] effect a constitution in which the will of the nation shall have an organized control over the actions of its government, and its citizens a regular protection against its oppressions."

Daniel Webster (1851): "Hold on, my friends, to the Constitution, and to the Republic for which it stands. Miracles do not cluster and what has happened once in 6,000 years, may not happen again. Hold onto the Constitution, for if the American Constitution should fail, there will be anarchy throughout the world."

Abraham Lincoln (1864): "I see in the near future a crisis approaching that unnerves me and cause me to tremble for the safety of my country… corporations have been enthroned and an era of corruption in high places will follow, and the money power of the country will endeavor to prolong its reign by working upon the prejudices of the people until all wealth is aggregated in a few hands and the Republic is destroyed."

The Bill of Rights

On March 4, 1789, the United States Congress convened in New York to consider amendments to the Constitution. Ten amendments — approved by that Congress — were ratified December 15, 1791 in what is known today as the Bill of Rights.

The Bill of Rights set America apart for generations. Countless people sought the freedom and security of this great nation. To lose one right — even one — is to lose a fortune. When rights are lost, they are extremely difficult to regain. It therefore is incumbent upon all Americans to do everything in their power to make sure these rights are preserved, protected and never, ever abolished

Respect and learn these precious amendments to the US Constitution, the Bill of Rights:

Amendment I
Congress shall make no law respecting an establishment of religion, or prohibiting the free exercise thereof, or abridging the freedom of speech, or of the press, or the right of the people to peacefully assemble, and to petition the Government for a redress of grievances.

Amendment II
A well-regulated militia, being necessary to the security of a free state, the right of the people to keep and bear arms shall not be infringed.

Amendment III
No soldier shall, in time of peace, be quartered in any house, without the consent of the owner, nor in time of war, but in a manner to be prescribed by law.

Amendment IV
The right of the people to be secure in their persons, houses, papers and effects, against unreasonable searches and seizures, to not be violated, and no warrants shall issue, but upon probable cause, supported by Oath or affirmation, and particularly describing the place to be searched, and the persons or things to be seized.

Amendment V
No person shall be held to answer for a capital, or otherwise infamous crime, unless on a presentment or indictment of a Grand Jury, except in cases arising in the land or naval forces, or in the militia, when in actual service in time of

war or public danger, nor shall any person be subject for the same offence to be put in jeopardy of life or limb; nor shall be compelled in any criminal case to be a witness against himself, nor be deprived of life, liberty, or property, without due process of law, nor shall private property be taken for public use, without just compensation.

Amendment VI

In all criminal prosecutions, the accused shall enjoy the right to a speedy and public trial, by an impartial jury of the State and district wherein the crime shall have been committed, which district shall have been previously ascertained by law, and to be informed of the nature and cause of the accusation; to be confronted with the witnesses against him; to have compulsory process for obtaining witnesses in his favor; and to have the Assistance of Counsel for his defense.

Amendment VII

In suits at common law, where the value in controversy shall exceed twenty dollars, the right of trial by jury shall be preserved and no fact tried by a jury, shall be otherwise re-examined in any Court of the United States, than according to the rules of the common law.

Amendment VIII

Excessive bail shall not be required, nor excessive fines imposed, nor cruel and unusual punishments inflicted.

Amendment IX

The enumeration of the Constitution, of certain rights, shall not be construed to deny or disparage others retained by the people.

Amendment X

The powers not delegated to the United States by the Constitution, or prohibited by it to the States, are reserved to the States respectively, or to the people.

Dark Influences on American Foreign Policy

Those who cast dark shadows in the Bush II Administration are not just those appointed to serve him, but those who, primarily from the outside, manipulate domestic and foreign policy to the detriment of national well being and international respect.

The four examples of dark influences — Henry Kissinger, Zbigniew Brzezinski, Ariel Sharon and Prince Bandar — further their own shadowy agendas, regardless who occupies the Oval Office. In the Bush II Administration, however, these ominous figures have enjoyed field days of opportunity unlike any other time.

Lyndon LaRouche, international economic and political genius, qualifies three of these men — Kissinger, Brzezinksi and Sharon — as global fascists, who would "rather destroy the universe than suffer any setbacks to the cause of their own lunatic ideologies."

HENRY KISSINGER

What can we say? Henry Kissinger's record on war crimes alone gives him an honored place in our nation's Gallery of Rogues. In some circles, he has earned the dark title of "Ariel Sharon of America." Although most of his nefarious activities took place during the Nixon administration (Watergate crimes), as well as the Reagan and Bush I Administrations, he still influences foreign policy. He is a member of the Defense Policy Board in the Pentagon under George W. He consistently advocated the bombing of Iraq.

Kissinger's war crimes include supporting mass murders in Southeast Asia, a dictatorship in Chile, and benefiting by investments in war-torn Yugoslavia. He cannot travel to several countries, for fear of being arrested and tried for war crimes.

One must not gloss over a life of war crimes where Kissinger is concerned. In his service to America as National Security Adviser from 1969-1973 and as Secretary of State from 1973-1977, he was complicit in many operations that resulted in hundreds of thousands of deaths and covert spying on Americans he deemed suspicious.

In 1969, Kissinger and President Nixon authorized the "secret" bombing of Cambodia, which continued openly for four additional years. US B-52s devastated that tiny country and caused hundreds of thousands of civilian deaths.

Kissinger and Nixon did not confine their destructive ways to Cambodia. In Viet Nam, devastation went on without mercy for years, but the December 1972 "Christmas bombing" of North Viet Nam was brutal. In just two weeks' time, the United States dropped more than 20,000 tons of bombs on military and civilian targets. The attack left 750,000 peasants dead and the Cambodian society in ruin. It set the stage for the rise to power of dictator Pol Pot, who later killed another million and a half Cambodians. The US attack was unnecessary, as peace terms, already outlined the previous October, were the same as those that the US accepted a month later, in January 1973.

Cambodia and Viet Nam were still not enough to satisfy the destructive desires of Kissinger. During Gerald Ford's presidency, he and Kissinger gave the nod in December 1975 to invade Indonesia and occupy East Timor.

In the next 25 years, more than a quarter of a million people died from illegal executions, torture and starvation; in just the first 18 months, as many as 80,000 civilians died. Of course, with complicity in such wanton devastation comes denial, and Kissinger was no exception regarding East Timor.

As is typical in many of these situations, the one person who should face trial for war crimes instead receives a reward. In the case of Kissinger and East Timor, he received a plum: a seat on the board of the US corporation that runs the world's largest gold mining operation there.

Kissinger went on to cause untold deaths and commit war crimes in Bangladesh, Chile and Cyprus, to name a few. He toppled democratically elected President Pinochet in Chile.

In characteristic disdain for the average person, Kissinger once referred to military men and women as "dumb, stupid animals to be used" as pawns for foreign policy.

Kissinger spoke at a Bilderberger Group meeting in Evian, France on May 21, 1992. Unbeknownst to him, a Swiss delegate taped his remarks. They forecast events that would transpire almost 10 years later in America.

> *Today Americans would be outraged if UN troops entered Los Angeles to restore order; tomorrow they will be grateful. This is especially true if they were told there was an outside threat from beyond, whether real or promulgated, that threatened our very existence. It is then that all the peoples of the world will plead with world leaders to deliver them from this evil. The one thing every man fears is the unknown. When presented with this scenario, individual rights will be willingly relinquished for the guarantee of their well being granted to them by their world government.*

Soon after the 9/11 attacks, victims' families and the public demanded an investigation. Bush stalled. Finally, he could no longer hold off public demand. He turned to the dark master of secrecy, appointing none other than Henry Kissinger to lead the Commission investigating those tragedies. Fortunately, enough public pressure came to bear, and Kissinger refused the post.

ZBIGNIEW BRZEZINSKI

When Zbigniew Brzezinski served as President Jimmy Carter's National Security Advisor, he seemed to have the best interests of the nation at heart. Looks are often deceiving. Behind the scenes, Brzezinski writes imperatives for American survival.

The most outrageous notion in his tome *Clash of Civilizations* is that to survive, the United States must conquer, especially Eurasia, which holds three-fourths of the world's people and resources. Lyndon LaRouche calls that plan "geopolitical lunacy."

In his master plan written more than 20 years ago, Brzezinski noted that the problem was that Americans do not take kindly to crusades of global conquest. The solution: A sudden, terrifying threat.

Could 9/11 have been that threat? Consider what happened immediately after 9/11. George Bush's ratings flew through the roof. People waved flags and rallied behind the President's call for war on terrorism. A sympathetic world added its support. A single series of threats on America's soil propelled this nation forward, all according to Brzezinski's master plan.

Brzezinksi's plan of world conquest has served as one of the bibles of the neocons pulling the strings in the Bush II Administration, all with Bush's enthusiastic approval.

ARIEL SHARON

Every time someone says that Israel is our only friend in the Middle East, I can't help but think that before Israel, we had no enemies in the Middle East.
Fr. John Sheehan, a Jesuit priest

In a contest to determine the Number One Terrorist in the world today, Ariel Sharon would win hands-down. His arrogance in crushing and oppressing the Palestinians with impunity alone warrants him that title.

His massacre of Palestinian refugees at Sabra and Shatila — and his willingness to destroy all Arabs at the expense of Israel — make him the modern-day equivalent of Stalin and Hitler. As the latest in a long line of Israeli leaders, who snub UN resolutions in order to further the Zionist agenda, Sharon blatantly violates human rights to advance his goals of expelling Palestinians and expanding the land of Israel.

The Zionist movement, created on May 14, 1948, was supposed to create Israel as an independent state for Jewish people. Instead, the Zionist State — a secular state, not one founded on Judaism — became a dependent entity that siphons billions of dollars annually from American taxpayers. No strings attached. This phenomenon occurs largely through AIPAC, the Israeli lobby that virtually controls all three branches of the US federal government.

This is no idle statement. On October 3, 2001, Sharon said, "We, the Jewish people, control America, and the Americans know it." Unfortunately, not enough people know that, and many people who do know it confuse Jews with Zionists. Many great Jewish people, who live by their religious laws and morals, have contributed mightily to the goodness of the world and to the United States. They should not be confused with Zionists, motivated by greed and domination, at any cost, not religion. Zionists follow the secular laws set forth in the Talmud. Jews, who practice Judaism, follow the teachings of the Torah and abhor oppression of the Palestinians.

The Israel of today is not the Israel of Biblical days. The Israel today is a secular — non-religious — State. Unfortunately, the right-wing fundamental Christians who support George W. Bush do not understand that. They are emotionally tied to Israel, simply because they read that name in their Bibles. They do not realize that that was then and this is now.

It is appropriate to note here that the events of 9/11 fell on an anniversary of a significant act of Zionist deception: the Lavon Affair, a false flag operation in which Israelis posed as Arabs working in Egypt. Their plot to bomb several buildings, including a US diplomatic office, backfired when one bomb exploded prematurely, injuring one of the bombers and bringing the arrest of the others, an Israeli spy ring. As is customary in these situations, the Zionists cried anti-Semitism, but truth won out when the scandal brought about the demise of Israeli Defense Minister Pinhas Lavon.

Although the plot failed, it unmasked the operations of the Mossad, Israel's CIA, who live by the motto, "By way of deception, thou shalt do war." It was not Israel's only attempt to deceive their way into war. It will not be their last.

Other crimes deceptively perpetrated by Israel include the bombing of the King David Hotel carried out by Israelis dressed as Arabs, the fake radio messages that tricked President Ronald Reagan into bombing Libya, and the unsuccessful attempt to sink the USS Liberty and blame it on Egypt. The pattern established in these crimes indicates possible Israeli complicity in the bombing of the USS Cole in Yemen and the 9/11 attacks on America.

More than ever before, Ariel Sharon's control of American foreign policy is obvious. Among his latest puppet-mastering acts involved his demand to prevail in Israel's proposed withdrawal from Gaza in exchange for expanding the West Bank settlements. Sharon threw a temper tantrum before leaving Israel, demanding that Bush give him everything he wanted or he would not pay him a visit.

George W capitulated and, in the process, trashed international law that guaranteed Palestinian refugees the Right of Return, ignored a handful of UN resolutions and, with the same handshake, waived recognition of a Palestinian state within the 1967 borders. Sharon got what he wanted. He always does. The American taxpayer picks up the tab, as it has for many years.

Under extreme pressure, including a letter signed by more than 50 US diplomats, who labeled Bush's endorsement of Sharon's plan as dangerous to US foreign policy in the Middle East, Bush withdrew his support of Sharon's plan. A day later, he angered the Arab world all over again by stating that the 2005 schedule for Palestinian statehood might not happen then.

Many Middle East experts insist that the only way the problem will be resolved in that regional hotbed will be a peaceful resolution to the Israeli-Palestinian issue. Of course, that would require an even-handed policy, which with the Bush II Administration full of pro-Israelis is unlikely to happen any time soon.

People like Marine General Anthony C. Zinni (Ret.), US Senator Ernest Hollings (D-SC) and former US Congressman Paul Findley expose the pervasive power of Israel in the United States, including dictating when we go to war and whom we attack. As Zinni said on May 14, 2004, "I couldn't believe what I was hearing about the benefits of this strategic move — that the road to Jerusalem [i.e., to an Israeli-Palestinian peace] led through Baghdad, when just the opposite is true."

Throughout the history of Zionism, its leaders maintained the same mantra issued by Ariel Sharon today. Consider these chilling quotes from former leaders of Israel:

Let us not ignore the truth among ourselves, politically we are the aggressors and they defend themselves. The country is theirs, because they inhabit it, whereas we want to come here and settle down, and in their view we want to take away from them their country.
– David Ben Gurion, 1938.

We must use terror, assassination, intimidation, land confiscation, and the cutting of all social services to rid the Galilee of its Arab population.
– David Ben Gurion, 1948.

There is no such thing as a Palestinian people. It is not as if we came and threw them out and took their country. They didn't exist.
– Golda Meir, Prime Minister of Israel, 1969.

How can we return the occupied territories? There is nobody to return them to.
– Golda Meir, 1969.

Jewish villages were built in the place of Arab villages. You do not even know the names of these Arab villages, and I do not blame you because geography books no longer exist. Not only do the books not exist; the Arab villages are not there either. There is not a single place built in this country [Israel] that did not have a former Arab population.
– Ben Gurion, 1978.

Palestinians are beasts walking on two legs.
– Manachem Begin, Prime Minister of Israel, 1982.

We have to kill all the Palestinians unless they are resigned to live here as slaves.
– Chairman Heilbrun of the Committee for the Re-election of General Shlomo Lahat, the Mayor of Tel Aviv, October 1983.

Israel will create in the course of the next 10 or 20 years conditions which would attract natural and voluntary migration of the refugees from the Gaza Strip to the west Bank of Jordan.
– Yitzhak Rabin, Prime Minister of Israel, 1983, describing his plan for ethnic cleansing of the occupied territory.

The Palestinians would be crushed like grasshoppers.
– Yitzhak Shamir, Prime Minister of Israel, 1988.

Israel should have exploited the repression of the demonstrations in China, when world attention focused on that country, to carry out mass expulsions among the Arabs of the territories.
– Benjamin Netanyahu, Israeli Deputy Foreign Minister, 1989.

The past leaders of our [Zionist] movement left us a clear message to keep Israel from the Sea to the River Jordan — for future generations — and for the Jewish people, all of whom will be gathered into this country.
– Yitzhak Shamir, 1990.

The settlement of the Land of Israel is the essence of Zionism. Without settlement, we will not fulfill Zionism. It's that simple.
– Yitzhak Shamir, 1997.

There is no Zionism, colonialization or Jewish State without the eviction of the Arabs and the expropriation of their lands.
– Ariel Sharon, Israeli Foreign Minister, 1998.

Everybody has to move, run, grab as many hilltops as they can to enlarge the settlements because everything we take now will stay ours. Everything we don't grab will go to them.
– Ariel Sharon, Israeli Foreign Minister, November 15, 1998

If we thought that instead of 200 Palestinian fatalities, 2,000 dead would put an end to the fighting at a stroke, we would use much more force.
– Ehud Barak, Prime Minister of Israel, 2000.

Israel may have the right to put others on trial, but certainly no one has the right to put the Jewish people and the State of Israel on trial.
– Ariel Sharon, Prime Minister of Israel, 2001.

The last quote demonstrates an interesting technique used by Ariel Sharon. It is to make the world believe that Jews and Israeli Zionists are synonymous. In reality, that assumption fosters unwarranted criticism of the multitude of Jews in Israel and around the world who do not support the agenda of Ariel Sharon.

The United States government gives Israel $3.5 billion in direct subsidies each year and another $12 billion in annual loan guarantees, which the Congress handily forgives later or provides Israel with the money to make payments. [That is like you taking out a bank loan and the bank forgiving your loan or giving you the money to make payments to the bank!] In total, Israel has cost the United States taxpayer FOUR TIMES the cost of the entire Apollo Moon Program.

There are no strings attached to the billions that we give Israel each year. We provide military equipment, which Israel turns around and sells to other countries. They use our weapons, our guns and bullets, to kill innocent Palestinians. We, the American taxpayers who foot these bills, have no say-so otherwise.

Sharon's recent defeat by his own Likud Party regarding unilateral withdrawal from Gaza fired up his arrogance and lust for more Palestinian blood. His incursion into Gaza, destroying buildings, lives, and even a small zoo, engendered world outrage, but he did not stop until he finished what he set out to do.

In the process, Sharon's Israel became all the things that Iraq was supposed to have been to justify the US invasion in March 2003 — defying the UN, killing and torturing its people, and amassing weapons of mass destruction. In his move on Gaza, Sharon undermined all legitimacy for our presence in Iraq.

Slowly, ever so slowly, the American people are starting to realize that the United States launched an illegal war against Iraq for Israel, as much as it did for oil. Did we comply out of concern for the security of the State of Israel, or because Israel continued to blackmail Bush II about 9/11?

PRINCE BANDAR

Prince Bandar — known formally as Prince Bandar bin Sultan — has served as Saudi Arabia's shadow diplomat to the United States under four presidents over the past 20 years.

During the Reagan years, Bandar earned the dubious distinction as an intermediary to the Iran-Contra scandal. He facilitated $32 million in Saudi funds for the Nicaraguan Contras. He courted the favor of then-Vice-President George H. W. Bush, appreciative that Bush did not automatically endorse Israel's agenda. He was a vital connection to Saudi King Fahd, until a stroke recently incapacitated him.

When George H. W. Bush (Bush I) was President, Bandar enjoyed close ties, almost as if he were one of the Bush family. When Iraq invaded Kuwait, the United States protected Saudi Arabia's borders during Desert Storm, and the Saudi royal family, out of appreciation, strengthened its ties to Washington. One little word connects the Bushes and Saudis: oil.

Bandar almost left his diplomatic post in Washington when his good friend, Bush I, lost to Bill Clinton in 1992. His ties to Clinton, however, began while Clinton was still Governor of Arkansas, when Bandar helped fund a center for Middle East studies at the University of Arkansas.

Although the two maintained a good relationship after Clinton became President, Bandar disagreed with much of the Clinton foreign policy and worked hard to influence it. Clinton used Bandar to set up an essential peace summit with Syrian President Assad, which failed, as did Camp David dialogue between Israel and the Palestinians. Although tension resulted between the Clinton Administration and Bandar over both incidents, Clinton continued to tap Bandar to aid in further peace initiatives.

Saudi Arabia held high expectations for George W. Bush, and Bandar approved the team he assembled. The Middle East went through serious changes, however, with the election of Ariel Sharon in 2001. Bandar made certain that the Bush II Administration knew that much more was at stake than Chairman Arafat. The entire Middle East was tense. Saudi Crown Prince

Abdullah, an advocate for the Palestinians, posed a problem, as Bandar had not fully supported the Palestinian cause.

In August 2001, Abdullah ordered Bandar to inform the Bush Administration that Saudi Arabia would protect their national interests from that day forward. Saudi policy dramatically shifted. The Bush II Administration's acquiescence to Israel regarding the Palestinians did not set well with the Crown Prince.

Bandar delivered the message to Condoleezza Rice, who hours later sent an appeasing message with Bandar to the Crown Prince — that the ties between the United States and Saudi Arabia were permanent. George W voiced support for a Palestinian state, a move that pleased the Crown Prince. Plans were quickly underway to revive the peace process and for George W to take the lead by announcing his support of a Palestinian state.

Bandar's connections then suffered a serious blow. Soon after the attacks of 9/11, he learned that 15 of the hijackers were Saudis. Bush and Bandar met and soon afterward, Bandar helped evacuate members of the bin Laden family from the United States. This action posed serious legal problems, because as relatives of the accused, Osama bin Laden, they should have faced questioning, as is the norm in criminal justice situations.

Prince Bandar again showed his closeness to Bush II, particularly regarding US for plans for Iraq War II (Oil War II, as some choose to call it). In a recent exposure in Robert Woodward's book, *Plan of Attack*, Bandar knew about the pre-emptive strike against Iraq before Secretary of State Colin Powell knew, although both parties did some fancy footwork to "correct" the facts.

Saudi Arabia is a wealthy country, and its royal family powerful in its control over other nations, including the United States, even to the point of manipulating oil prices to influence our presidential elections. The two countries satisfied each other's national interests — oil for the United States and military arms and protection for Saudi Arabia.

Prince Bandar, through an unprecedented (oil) pipeline to the White House, has served as Saudi Arabia's primary negotiator. Folks in some circles consider Bandar the most dangerous man in Washington.

The hidden agendas of these individuals have spawned illegal activities, pre-emptive wars, rejection of international law, war crimes, and ruinous domestic policies against the American people — and people of other countries.

The Bush Dynasty

Every dynasty, characterized by the powerful rule of a single family through generations, has inauspicious beginnings. The Bush dynasty, with its own dark and shady history, is no exception.

Roots of the Bush family tree extend back to England, but the most ominous roots are firmly entrenched in an exclusive Yale society, known as Skull & Bones, incorporated in 1856. Other aliases include The Order by insiders and Chapter 322 of a similar secret society in Germany, and The Brotherhood of Death.

Regardless of the name, its members, sworn to secrecy and silence, comprise an elite, powerful, and wealthy fraternity with single vision — world domination by the elite. Skull & Bones members dominate government, financial institutions and corporations, as many as 800 at any one time in America.

Skull & Bones membership peppers the Bush family. Grandfathers, uncles, fathers, sons and brothers, they bear the ominous trademark of secrecy that underscores their nefarious activities, hypocrisy and greed.

SAMUEL PRESCOTT BUSH

Samuel Prescott Bush was George W's paternal great grandfather. His claim to fame, as part of the Bush dynasty, was his participation in the "Merchants of Death", a ring of evil arms dealers who caused wars, during World War I.

He laid the foundation for the Bush dynasty in America, one that would wend its way through opium smuggling, money laundering, and many other scandalous activities at home and abroad.

In the spring of 1918, he served as chief of the Ordnance, Small Arms and Ammunition Section of the War Industries Board. He was a close advisor to President Herbert Hoover.

Sam and his wife, Flora Sheldon, were parents of Prescott Bush, Sr., who was George W's grandfather.

GEORGE HERBERT "BERT" WALKER

Banking was in George Herbert Walker's blood. He served as president of Brown Brothers Harriman, the largest private investment bank in the United States back in the 1930s and 1940s.

Skull & Bonesmen dominated that bank, but the rise of the bank to the top came through a powerful Jewish banking monopoly, which provided considerable funding for Adolph Hitler's extermination process. Walker was one of Adolph Hitler's most powerful supporters in the United States.

Before that, Brown Brothers funded slave plantations during the Civil War, and one of its former partners, a Bank of England official, was Hitler's most avid supporter.

George Herbert Walker founded the banking and investment firm known as G. H. Walker & Company.

George Herbert Walker was the maternal great grandfather of George W.

PRESCOTT BUSH, SR.

Father of George Herbert Walker Bush or Bush I, Prescott Bush served as vice president of Brown Brothers Harriman. An ambitious person, he was also director of the Holland-American Trading Corporation and the Seamless Steel Equipment Corporation, fronts for Nazi operations in World War II.

Prescott also served as Director of the Harriman Fifteen Corporation. As Director of Union Bank, Prescott handled the Nazi money-laundering machine.

Prescott's associates were, on the surface, pillars of their communities, but behind the scenes were involved in some of the world's great scandals. John Foster Dulles, who later became Secretary of State, served as attorney to I. G. Farben, an enormous Nazi industrial trust that, among other things, created Auschwitz. Farben and others participated in covering up John Kennedy's assassination, supplying ethyl lead to the Nazis, pardoning hundreds of Nazi war criminals, and bringing Nazi doctors to the United States to conduct scientific experiments on innocent American civilians.

In 1940, Farben built a huge plant at Auschwitz concentration camp, using slave labor. Standard Oil paid for the SS guards of the camp. William Stamps Farish, president and CEO of Standard Oil of New Jersey, served as controller of the global Farben-Standard Oil cartel. One of the richest men in Texas, Farish is George Bush's "closest friend and confidant." Nice friend.

Some of the fortunes of George Herbert Walker Bush and his brothers came from the Bush family's complicity in the operations at Auschwitz. That is just one fact you will not find in Bush I's official biography.

Prescott fell from his financial mountaintop in 1942, when the US government used the Trading with the Enemy Act to seize all of the Nazi banking operations conducted by Prescott. Although the action depleted some of his wealth, he managed to pass on an Auschwitz death camp fortune to his sons. Prescott went on to be a United States Senator from Connecticut in 1952, but the preceding events had tarnished the family's honor.

Prescott Bush, Sr. and his wife, Dorothy Walker, had five children, including one a daughter, Nancy, and another son, Jonathan. For our purposes here, we will examine the career paths of three of his sons.

PRESCOTT BUSH, JR.

Uncle Prescott, another in the long line of Yale graduates, currently serves as Chairman of the US-China Chamber of Commerce and as president of Prescott Bush Resources. His close ties to China started seven years after his brother George Herbert Walker, ended his Nixon-appointed ambassadorship there. He built the first golf course in China, located in Shanghai, with help from the Japanese. He has known the former Chinese President, Jiang Zemin since Zemin was Mayor of Shanghai.

During his many trips to China, he entered a business relationship with none other than the richest man in China, Rong Yiren, a former trade minister. Bush family connections to China surely helped him secure lucrative business deals with that country, such as partnership with the Japanese-owned Aoki in 1988 or the American Asset Management Company that eluded US sanctions and shipped satellites to China.

Even the Tiananmen Square massacre failed to stop Prescott from traveling to China to further his business interests. After all, business is business and human rights violations are, well, you know. How fortunate that China is ripe for plucking business deals and desperate for jobs. It seems like the perfect set-up for outsourcing opportunities, and Prescott Bush, Jr. holds the right position to facilitate and promote those opportunities.

Prescott brokered deals that netted him tidy sums, aided his brother George in a variety of illegal covert operations and spied on President Jimmy Carter for the Reagan/Bush ticket. That is what brothers are for, isn't it?

WILLIAM H. T. "BUCKY" BUSH

A director on the Board of Engineered Support Systems, Inc. that supplies high-tech military goods wherever they are needed, William Bush has made a bundle on both Iraqi wars and to high bidders around the globe. In 2003, the company sold $13 million in high-tech radar equipment to upgrade fighter jets for communist China. The Bush-China connection — dating back to Grandpa's opium smuggling days — is especially close. More about that as we progress.

Like other family members before him, William Bush's priorities rest on greedy acquisition at the expense of others. He apparently sees nothing wrong in propping up a communist regime that racks up human rights abuses, invades neighbors and has its own caches of WMD.

For George W's Oil War II in Iraq and Homeland Security Department, William, affectionately known as Uncle Bucky, has raked in millions. For the Pentagon, his company, ESS, developed mobile sheds that provide command centers and field hospitals for non-contaminated areas of operation. The six companies that comprise the ESS holding company and that supply the US military with everything from faucets to tanks have made the greatest gain from the Iraq War.

When Homeland Security Chief Tom Ridge tried to trigger mass paranoia here at home with his threat level color change chart, Uncle Bucky came to the rescue. His company developed a fleet of mobile communication centers in the event al-Qaeda threw Americans a germ warfare curve. What is a little scare now and then if your uncle makes a fat bundle?

In all, William Bush's company has made approximately $380 million in 2003 from just the Pentagon. That's substantially more than the $297-plus million in 2001. Then there was the China deal and Homeland Security deal, and millions more from a deal with Saudi Arabia. Did Uncle Bucky have to outbid other contractors for all the deals he has made for the War on Terrorism?

Although we would like to feel assured that George W did not wage war to fatten his uncle's bank account, we know that profits from war have come handily for the Bush Dynasty.

GEORGE HERBERT WALKER BUSH (BUSH I)

We have a political system that awards office to the most ruthless, cunning and selfish of mortals, then act surprised when those willing to do anything to win power are equally willing to do anything with it.
Mike Rivero, whatreallyhappened.com

George Bush I's official biography shows a stellar career with barely room to inscribe between the lines all the shady operations he ran at various levels of power. After all, the sinister dynasty bloodlines run through him.

At every point in his career, one does not have to look far to find discrepancies in his showcase of great public deeds and "Points of Light" speeches. Starting with this service in the Navy, one wonders if he joined to serve the nation or to restore the Bush family honor after the US government seized his father's banking operations.

Bush received a medal of heroism despite the fact that the plane he was flying when shot down would have withstood a crash landing in the sea. Bush bailed out, leaving his two comrades to die. Nevertheless, he received medals of honor and heroism for his military service.

Bush attended Yale, where in his junior year Skull & Bones tapped him and 14 others for initiation into the secret society. Like grandfather and father, like son. Even Phi Beta Kappa, in which he was a member, has origins that pre-date S&B. While at Yale, he married Barbara Pierce, and they had six children, although one died in childhood.

With graduation came a lucrative career in the oil industry in Texas, where he first developed a personal interest in politics. Bush met Richard Nixon in 1946 through Prescott Bush. He served as a US Congressman for two terms, then ran twice for the US Senate, but failed both times.

In 1960, Bush became Nixon's protege during his campaign for the presidency against John F. Kennedy. Bush was a top agent at the CIA by then. He recruited Cubans for the Bay of Pigs invasion, because of the Bush family's oil interests in that region through their Zapata Petroleum Company. Bush let the CIA use Zapata as a front for offshore drilling platforms and other operations. Zapata was one of Cuban President Batista's main suppliers.

When Kennedy failed to provide air cover at Bay of Pigs, Nixon and Bush openly discussed killing Kennedy. Bush disputes the charge and denies working for the CIA until 1975, but evidence indicates that he was complicit in recruiting Lee Harvey Oswald for the assassination of President John F. Kennedy.

Along the way, Bush met Felix Rodriguez, who was with the CIA in Mexico. Rodriguez later became Bush's link to Oliver North's Contra drug-for-guns operations when Bush served as Reagan's Vice President. Networking!

With all his connections and Nixon as a mentor, Bush won appointments to a number of top-drawer positions — Ambassador to the United Nations, Chairman of the Republican Party, and Ambassador to China. Bush served as Director of the CIA from 1975-76, appointed by President Gerald Ford. In 1980, he ran for President but when he lost, Ronald Reagan made him Vice President, handing him the responsibilities of Federal deregulation and anti-drug programs, which he ran for eight years.

Of course, his biography fails to note that the War on Drugs has been a travesty from the start. The CIA ran smalltime drug dealers out of business but not the giant drug cartels.

One need not look far from Bush's nose to find illegal use of drug money. One of his chief aides served as the conduit between the Contras and the White House. Oliver North noted more than 500 times in his journals that drug money was used to support contra operations. Bush denied knowledge of the Contras, but in 1992, *TIME* magazine reported that he likely played a part in the 1986-88 arms-for-hostages swap in the Iran-Contra scandal.

As a former CIA director, Bush had to know what was going on, but readily issued denials because the facts certainly did not mesh with his public anti-drug persona. He had been fighting the War on Drugs since Nixon first appointed him to the White House Cabinet Committee on International Narcotics Control in 1971.

In 1988, Bush won his party's nod for President. In his acceptance speech, he asserted, "I want a drug-free America. Tonight, I challenge the young people of our country to shut down the drug dealers around the world. My Administration will be telling the dealers, 'Whatever we have to do, we'll do, but your day is over. You're history.'" One wonders how he was able to say all that with his tongue firmly planted in his cheek.

When his campaign for President was in full swing and he was stumping his way as a "family values" candidate, embarrassing news surfaced. An expose named seven members of his campaign as fascist, pro-Nazi, anti-Semite members of the GOP's Heritage Group Council. Part of this private funding circle comprised of extreme right-wing Eastern European émigrés (like those Dulles brought here after World War II), they later resigned or were fired. One of Bush's associates had been responsible for killing 100,000 Jews, according to Nazi records.

George H. W. Bush became the 41st President of the United States and quickly reaffirmed his goal of winning the War on Drugs. In the shadows lurked Bush's involvement in cracking down on small-time drug dealers, all the while helping to organize a Colombian cartel with ties back to 1981. At a meeting of the cartel that year, the CIA urged the 200 or so drug dealers to consolidate under CIA protection by kidnapping certain Colombian drug lords, an activity for which the CIA paid a group three million dollars.

That was not the only time the CIA worked in drug trafficking. Sources on record note that Manuel Noriega and the Mossad (Israeli Intelligence) handled drug deals with the CIA throughout Central and South America. A CIA chief in Miami set up drug trafficking from those regions into the United States. That same Miami chief later became Bush's Associate Deputy Director of Operations, number three at the CIA. Although fired, he later surfaced in time to play a significant role in the Iran-Contra scandal when Bush was Vice President under Reagan.

These facts come as no surprise to anyone who has even marginal knowledge about the War on Drugs. Most people know that the US government has been complicit in providing heroin and cocaine, including crack cocaine and other drugs to dealers and addicts on the streets and in corporate offices across America. For President George H. W. Bush to publicly crack down on drugs and drug trafficking smacks of hypocrisy almost beyond comprehension.

Countless other stories prevail about Bush and his role in the business of drugs and the world's leading drug dealers. With drug trafficking came secret drug funds outside the United States and secret drug flights into the US.

Some of the operations — such as money laundering and even murder — ran with the full cooperation of organized crime.

From 1987 to 1991, as Vice-President and then as President, Bush headed the South Florida Task Force and later chaired the National Narcotics Interdiction System, both set up to "stem" the flow of drugs into the United States. During Bush I's reign as the nation's drug czar, cocaine smuggling into the US tripled.

Some individuals who had worked for the CIA openly admitted knowledge of Bush's involvement in drug trafficking, particularly in the Iran-Contra operation. Frederick Kempe's *Divorcing the Dictator: America's Bungled Affair with Noriega* in 1990 documents the connection of Israel and the CIA to the Contra-cocaine operation in Central America.

> *Noriega, the new Comandante, made clear he was willing to be more cooperative than his predecessors. He was also feeling more heat for Panama's role in laundering money for international drug traffickers, and he interpreted a George Bush visit in December 1983 as an appeal for more help for the Contras. In Noriega's mind, he thought Bush was saying that if Panama helped the Contras it could diffuse criticism about money laundering.*

Bush met with Noriega several times and, despite the DEA's wishes to arrest him for drug trafficking of tons of cocaine into the United States through Panama, Bush kept him on the CIA payroll.

Bush ended his active anti-drug czar role in 1990 with an invasion of Panama known as Operation Just Cause, apparently to shut down President Noriega's drug trafficking (in which Bush and the CIA were complicit). In reality, Noriega had gotten too big for his britches, threatening Bush's extensive investments there. The goal was to install a new president, who would be more cooperative with Bush.

The invasion killed thousands of civilians, and 26 US soldiers, all to protect Bush's drug trafficking operations in Panama and his $350 millions in laundered investments with his brother Prescott's help.

Noriega landed in a US prison, but the money laundering operation through Panama's banks eventually grew to two-thirds higher volume than it was before the invasion. Sixty percent of the Panamanians who survived Operation Just Cause live in poverty, and 17 percent live in extreme poverty. Twenty-four percent of the people there suffer malnutrition. Where Bush was concerned, however, protecting his assets came first.

Bush later claimed executive privilege to avoid testifying in Oliver North's trial. In so doing, he became the first President to use executive privilege to keep his vice presidential activities a secret.

In addition to keeping a hectic drug trafficking schedule, President Bush helped trick the American people into supporting US protection of Kuwait after Saddam Hussein invaded that tiny kingdom rich in oil ruled by royal families. Although Kuwait had plenty of oil reserves of its own, it stole oil from its Iraqi neighbor. Then, in cooperation with the United Arab Emirates, they exceeded their oil production quotas, driving down oil prices and hitting Iraq, already set back $70 billion from the Iraq-Iran War, with billions in revenues.

When Kuwait failed to meet Iraq's simple demands, Saddam invaded. Citing what Bush called "naked aggression", he rallied the American people. "America stands where it always has, against aggression, against those who would use force to replace the rule of law." Interesting, considering his family backed Hitler, and he himself became the only head of state condemned by the World Court for the 'unlawful use of force.' Panama, Nicaragua, Argentina, Chile and Indonesia are a few, who felt the sharp end of the Bush stick.

In yet another example of blatant hypocrisy, Bush condemned big Iraq for invading little Kuwait, supposedly a no-no in the civilized world. Bush opted for war against Iraq, the country he had supported in its 10-year war against Iran, which claimed more than a million lives. The United States supported both sides of that war, just as the Bush family throughout history had supported Hitler and the Allies and other opposing parties, all for the almighty dollar.

Congressman Henry Gonzalez set the record straight. "The Bush administration sent US technology to the Iraqi military and to many Iraqi military factories, despite overwhelming evidence showing that Iraq intended to use the technology in its clandestine nuclear, chemical, biological and long-range missile programs."

The incubator fabrication, thanks to global public relations giant Hill & Knowlton, eventually fell apart, but it succeeded in helping Bush sell the first Iraq War to the American people.

The Pentagon proceeded to prepare for war by building a huge military installation in Saudi Arabia. The irony of Gulf War I is that Bush for a long time supported Saddam Hussein. Bush's Secretary of State, James Baker III, funneled a billion dollars in military aid, disguised as agricultural commodity loans. He did that, despite Hussein's boasts of having enough chemical weapons to destroy Israel.

The 325,000 troops Bush sent to Iraq met an additional 118,000 from other allied countries. In a 100-hour land battle, known as Desert Storm, which followed weeks of air bombardment, Iraq's army fell. The thrill of battle translated poorly at home, however, due to economic woes, high deficit spending and increased violence in inner cities.

Christopher Hitchens, columnist for *The Nation*, quoted Bush I speaking about so-called atrocities committed by Saddam Hussein:

> *No one can see the pictures or hear the accounts of this human suffering, men, women, and most painfully of all, innocent children, and not be deeply moved…We must do everything in our power to save innocent life, and this is the American tradition and we will continue to live up to that tradition.*

Hitchen then noted:

> *The 'American tradition' employed by Bush and his murdering minions like General Colin Powell and 'Stormin' Norman' Schwarzkopf, amounted to the unleashing of more bombs on both the military and civilian population of Iraq than was dropped by the Allies during World War II.*
>
> *These activities are just a sampling of the Bush family endeavors. What can one say about a man who makes brutal war on a sovereign country, killing thousands, just to protect his own drug trade? Or murders a million innocent children through war, starvation and disease to protest his and his cronies' oil interests? Or participates in perverted sexual activities with prostituted children? Or illegally smuggles tons of narcotics into the United States while publicly declaring to be 'anti-drug', releasing major drug traffickers while ordinary people possessing a little marijuana are sentenced to long jail terms? Such a man could only be considered the most evil of creatures…on a scale rivaling that of Hitler.*

In 1992, George Herbert Walker Bush lost the Presidency to William (Bill) Jefferson Clinton.

On January 18, 1993, just two days before his presidency ended, Bush granted clemency and freed Aslam Adam. A Pakistani, Adam served only eight years of a 55-year sentence for smuggling $1.5 million in cocaine into the United States and was not yet eligible for parole.

This section is not complete without a word about Barbara Bush, wife of George Herbert Walker Bush and mother of George W. Whatever else she has said or written faded into oblivion on March 18, 2003, when she appeared on 'Good Morning, America.' Regarding the launch of Iraq War II, she said, "But why should we hear about body bags and deaths, and how many, what day it's gonna happen, and how many this or what do you suppose? Or, I mean, it's, it's not relevant. So why should I waste my beautiful mind on something like that? And watch him suffer?" [Supposedly, the last remark referred to George W.] Methinks her pearls are too tight.

NEIL MALLON BUSH

Each member of the Bush dynasty owns up to his own specialty under the umbrella of fraud. Neil's specialty was real estate fraud — and being an embarrassment to the two presidents in the family.

Although dubbed "Mr. Perfect" at a young age because of his thoughtfulness, his career has been far from perfect. He overcame dyslexia and went on to receive a degree in international economics from Tulane University and an MBA. His career got a jumpstart soon after marrying Sharon Smith, a schoolteacher from New Hampshire, and moving to Denver, Colorado.

There, the charming and handsome son of the US Vice President met with approval by Denver's society. After a stint with Amoco, he quit and, with two former co-workers, formed JNB, an oil exploration company that never found anything worth drilling. But the Bush name opened doors, doubled his previous salary, and helped Neil raise millions, thanks to a couple of real estate fat cats, who would encounter him in his next stint.

In 1985, Neil joined the Board of Silverado Savings & Loan in Denver. Those real estate fat cats that had invested in JNB in part out of loans from Silverado poured money into Neil's account but did not repay Silverado. When Silverado's borrowers defaulted on millions in loans, some of it went to the Contras. Soon after Bush I became President, Silverado shut down, and the US taxpayers paid the one-billion-dollar tab.

For his role in the savings and loan scandal, Neil paid only $50,000 in answer to a lawsuit and received a slap on the hand. Of course, Neil continues to maintain his innocence.

All hopes for a political career dashed, Neil proceeded to secure lucrative deals as a business consultant for companies around the world, trading his name for fortunes. Often, he knew nothing about the businesses that hired him, but his name served those companies well. Whenever Neil ran into trouble along the way, one of Dad's rich friends bailed him out.

His current business, Ignite!, is an educational software company that he co-founded in 1999. Again, his name came in handy when he went to raise millions from American and foreign investors. In 2002, the company became partners with a Mexican company that resulted in a layoff of half of its employees and outsourcing their jobs to Mexico.

The most recent headlines involve Neil and his marriage, trashed by his wayward ways, ending in a scandalous divorce. Apparently, his ex appears ready to expose the Bush family.

JEB BUSH

Jeb Bush's specialty — other than rigging presidential elections — was oil and gas fraud. Like father, like son, Jeb helped his Vice President father by serving as a liaison with the Contras and helping set up an arms pipeline through Guatemala. He also has a knack for attracting business partners who break the law and go to prison.

In his connections with the Contra/Anti-Castro Cuban community in Florida, Jeb released from prison a Cuban-American terrorist, who was responsible for bombing a Cuban airliner in 1976, killing 73 people.

One of Jeb's acquaintances, Cuban-American drug trafficker, Leonel Martinez, contributed to Jeb's political ambitions and to his father's. Coincidentally, those contributions were made when Jeb was chairing the South Florida Drug Task Force and later the National Narcotics Interdiction System.

Twice in the 1980s, when Bush I was Vice President, Jeb lobbied for people involved in schemes designed to defraud the US government of millions of dollars. In 1991, he flew to Nigeria to meet with government officials there. His mission was to secure a deal whereby Nigeria would buy $74 million in water pumps from Jeb's Florida partner. To help secure the deal, he carried a couple of suitcases full of cash. Bribery is the name of the game in Nigeria.

In the months leading up to the 2000 presidential election, Florida Governor Jeb Bush and his Secretary of State Katherine Harris ordered the removal of 9,000 names from the voter registration rolls. Their reason was that they were the names of former felons. Ex-felons cannot vote in Florida. The truth of the matter emerged after the election. Ninety-seven percent of the names belonged to legally registered black voters, not to ex-felons.

Jeb is a member of PNAC, a tight group of neocons, who embrace a dark agenda of creating a New World Order through conquest and domination. Oh, yes, and amassing a fortune in oil, gold, whatever.

Among other things, PNAC — Richard Cheney, Donald Rumsfeld, Paul Wolfowicz, I. Lewis Libby, Richard Perle, and Jeb Bush — planned Oil War II, even before George W became president. They were smart enough to know that world conquest would be a hard sell and that it would take another Pearl Harbor to rally the troops. The events of 9/11 delivered.

The American Ali Baba
George W. Bush

*To announce that there must be no criticism of the President,
or that we are to stand by the President, right or wrong,
it is not only unpatriotic and servile,
but morally treasonable to the American public.*

Theodore Roosevelt
United States President, 1901-1909

Essentially, George W. Bush is not the 43rd President of the United States. He is a resident of the White House and we have seen him sitting behind the President's desk in the oval office. George W. Bush is a puppet in an administration run amok. He has fueled hatred and rendered the world unsafe for everyone.

For all the right wing fanatics and neocons who support him, he attracts more adversaries and critics than does any president in memory. Liberals and conservatives alike call for his impeachment. Veteran journalist, Helen Thomas, who has covered the White House news beat for seven presidents, admits that George W is the worst president she has ever known. She does not stand alone in that opinion. In short, Helen Thomas was right.

For the purpose of this book, we refer to him officially as President Bush II to differentiate from his father, Bush I. His official biography states that he became President in January 2001, but it neglects to inform the reader how he got there. It was not by promising everything to everyone. It was not by winning the hearts and minds of Americans. It was not by offering a better nation or safer world.

Albert Gore won the popular vote. All George Bush needed was a shady voting scandal in brother Jeb's backyard and the votes of five Supreme Court justices on a Saturday, when they normally do not meet. It pays to have friends in high places.

What qualified George W. Bush to be president in the first place? Had he served in the trenches, blazed trails as a pioneer in human services or fought injustices around the globe? Hardly. Let us start from the beginning.

Born in Connecticut in 1946, George W grew up in Texas, but returned to Connecticut to get his bachelor's degree at Yale — and his rightful place in Skull & Bones. He interrupted his education to join the Texas Air National Guard. Unlike his brave counterparts in Viet Nam and other hot spots around the globe, George went missing in action here in the States. His reputation for drug and alcohol addiction at the time was legend.

He ignored direct orders for duty and received assignment to a disciplinary unit in Denver. True to form, he failed to appear there, too.

In his autobiography, *A Charge to Keep,* in 1999, he said, "I continued flying with my unit for the next several years." In fact, officials suspended him from flight duty in August 1972 and did not allow him to fly again.

After his "service" in the Guard, he enrolled in the MBA program at Harvard Business School and received his degree in 1975.

He returned to Texas to launch a career in the oil industry. Like father, like son. George lost a bid for Congress, then used his own trust fund money, combined with that of his father's rich friends, to start his own gas and oil company, Arbusto Energy. One friend just happened to be the one-and-only US business connection for one of Osama bin Laden's brothers.

George fared no better than his brother Neil in exploration efforts, and more wealthy friends of Dad bought out Arbusto and gave George a healthy salary along with the CEO title for Spectrum 7 Energy Corporation.

Oil prices dipped in the mid-1980s, threatening to run energy companies aground, including Spectrum. George W negotiated with Harken Energy to buy Spectrum, with the end result finding George in a director's chair, pocketing $120,000 in salary and beefing up his portfolio with $600,000 in Harken stock. Of course, his name had nothing to do with all that.

Through a number of backdoor deals that crisscrossed the globe, Harken landed exclusive rights to drill for gas and oil in the Persian Gulf, although it would be Harken's first such venture overseas.

George W worked on his father's presidential campaign in 1988. After Bush I became the 41st President of the United States, George W formed a partnership and purchased the Texas Rangers baseball franchise. He served as the managing general partner of the team from 1989 until he became Governor in 1994.

Officially, his biography paints a glowing picture of his two terms as Governor of Texas, but reality paints a completely different picture. Instead of boldly taking initiative to improve schools, standards plummeted. Instead of giving tax breaks to everyone, he made sure his rich friends got a bigger piece of the pie.

His official position stated that he was committed to ushering in a responsible era in America. He called on all Americans to be "citizens, not spectators; citizens, not subjects; responsible citizens building communities of service and a nation of character". Maybe that played well in Texas, but even he could not live up to the standards he set.

Governor Bush's most notorious hallmark as Governor was that of overseeing more state-sponsored executions of prisoners — 152 — than has any other governor. His penchant for death dates back to his childhood when he put firecrackers into the mouths of frogs and blew them up. After Texas executed its first female prisoner in the state's history, Bush mocked her pleas for life on a television talk show.

George W entered the presidential race in 2000, and with the help of Karl Rove's dirty tricks, his brother Jeb's shenanigans in Florida, and votes from Supreme Court cronies, he became President. Dick Cheney, who had quit his CEO post at Halliburton to become Bush's Vice President, assembled a hard-core neocon group to run the Administration.

"The Bush Administration," according to Doug Henwood, editor of The Left Business Observer, "is a bunch of private sector alumni called upon to perform the task in government they were performing in the private sector."

The makeup of the Administration should have sounded alarms and raised red flags, because the agenda of the chosen neocons called for wars of conquest and the New World Order, whatever the cost. Bush's cavalier attitude about launching an illegal war, based largely on the lies of a criminal and endorsed by the neocons around him, rests in his self-assurance that God chose him to rule the world.

George W credits Rev. Billy Graham with converting his wayward ways to those of a true believer. One wonders if that is all the renowned evangelist taught George. After all, it was Graham, who on April 15, 1969, suggested to President Nixon that the United States bomb the dikes in North Vietnam. At Nixon's own estimate, that would have killed one million people.

The tragedies of 9/11 gave Bush and his people what they wanted — a cause that united (most) Americans and brought world sympathy to our shores. On September 20, 2001, Bush declared that any nation that sponsors, aids or harbors terrorists is an enemy of the United States. A year later, he issued a remarkable document entitled "National Security Strategy of the United States of America" in which he declared the right of the US to wage pre-emptive wars on rogue states.

In reality, Bush and his thieves used those events to launch a war in Afghanistan with immediate plans for a pre-emptive strike against Saddam Hussein's regime in Iraq. Their complicity in those events still draws intense public scrutiny and may force criminal charges.

First, our archenemy was Osama bin Laden, but then Bush's neocons successfully tied him to Saddam Hussein, and all of a sudden, there was reason to start another war. Actually, they hatched that plan long before Bush II became President. Anyway, war was the number one item on the neocon agenda. They want war and more war, until every "enemy" country adopts the American way — democracy. They forgot that democracy — like charity — begins at home.

In his zeal to appease right wing Christian fanatical supporters, he embraced Biblical scriptures that spoke of war instead of peace, hate instead of love. "Do not do an immoral thing for a moral reason," former President Warren Harding once said. Bush only thought his reason was moral, but he did an immoral deed. Most of the world knew it was wrong and staged protests larger than ever before in history. A solidarity peace movement galvanized in the wake of the war.

Throughout the war, Bush's thieves lied and deceived the American public, depleted public coffers to fund the war, embedded journalists to warp reporting from the front lines, and regularly injected the fear factor to keep his poll numbers up. Bush used 9/11 to authorize the shredding of the Bill of Rights through the Patriot Act I and in creation of the Homeland Security Department. Tom Ridge's color-changing codes told Americans when to watch out or the boogey man would get them. Too many jokes since then laid that warning system to rest. No one believes it anymore.

Bush made sure his rich friends got tax cuts, and manipulated laws to accommodate crony corporations. It did not matter that they violated environmental laws. At the same time he gave to the rich, he took from those who faced hard economic times, including America's youngest and strongest. He sent them to war, but denied them overtime pay, hurting their families back home. Bush plans to make additional cuts in veterans' benefits in 2005 and 2006, should he return to office.

In May 2003, he ceremoniously landed on a naval ship to pronounce the end of Oil War II. It really was just the beginning. More US troops and more Iraqis died after Bush declared the war over than before.

In April 2004, as Iraqis buried their dead in mass graves and prisoner abuse scandals surfaced, Bush made a presidential pronouncement. "We are not an imperial power…A secure and free Iraq is an historic opportunity to change the world…I fully understand the consequences of what we are doing. We're changing the world."

What have Americans received in exchange for trusting George W. Bush? War, scandalous torture of prisoners, international embarrassment, widespread hatred, increased danger to Americans around the world, a crumbling economy, and loss of most of our precious rights. Calls for his impeachment started long ago, led by such respected Constitutional authorities as former Attorney General Ramsey Clark.

"The United States is committed to the worldwide elimination of torture," said President George W. Bush, "and we are leading this fight by example. I call on all governments to join with the United States and the community of law-abiding nations in prohibiting, investigating, and prosecuting all acts of torture and in undertaking to prevent other cruel and unusual punishment."

The Bush Administration mastered the art of deception. Now, they must dine on their own words.

Then the prisoner abuse scandals broke, thanks to Seymour Hersch and "60 Minutes" — but, in great part, to the power of the Internet and alternative news sources that had millions one-upping mainstream media sources. Bush resolutely supported his Defense Secretary, the highest office of accountability, and his military officers at the highest levels. It was as if to tell Americans and the world that whatever happened "over there" does not require moral accountability. Nothing could be further from the truth. Bush and his 40 Thieves lied and deceived the American public — and the world — and the public must hold them all accountable.

Bush repeatedly wore blinders. On April 15, 2004, he said: "Our military is performing brilliantly. See, the transition from torture chambers and rape rooms and mass graves and fear of authority is a tough transition. And they're doing the good work of keeping this country stabilized as a political process unfolds."

The Bush Administration and elements of the American military hierarchy, the media and the corporate establishment are indictable for war crimes. They ordered, directed, propagated and profited from an illegal war in flagrant violation of international law. Since the war began in early 2003, more laws have been broken and more war crimes committed.

The only way to retake the country and save the Constitution is through the election process. Vote out all members of Congress and the Senate who support the war and Bush's illegal agenda. Vote out the President and Vice President, and his neocons will leave with him. Stop supporting sponsors of all media that feed Bush rhetoric instead of the truth.

Bush II, motivated by the same greed that drove his great grandfather, grandfathers, and father, once said that a dictatorship would be all right, as long as he was the dictator. Is terrorism inside the United States really from outside or is it homegrown to cause Americans to believe they have no choice but to surrender their rights and accept the totalitarian control of their new ruler. Or, as Ralph Nader refers to him, the "messianic militarist."

The neocons in the Bush II Administration desperately want to hold onto power and might stop at nothing to achieve their goals. If that means killing a million Americans to bring the remaining 280 million into line, they will find a way of doing that. Already, local authorities in several states captured Mossad agents in the midst of suspicious activities around US nuclear plants. Their identification and immigration papers proved false. Unlike other countries that prosecute such perpetrators, our government sends them directly back to Israel. What are they doing prowling around our nuclear plants? Who are those phony Israelis who pose as art peddlers and moving van operators?

Predictions abound that another attack on American soil is imminent. In order for Bush II's plummeting poll numbers to rise, an attack must happen far enough ahead of the November 2004 elections to matter. Bush has a back-up plan. If an attack occurs, he can declare martial law and disband the elections. The US Constitution, Declaration of Independence and Bill of Rights that served this country well for more than 200 years will end up in the dustbin of history. Bush would have his dictatorship.

His 40 Thieves

*The first method of estimating the intelligence
of a ruler is to look at the men he has around him.*

Niccolo Machiavelli
The Prince

Thievery comes in many disguises. It can be the petty pilfering of another person's private property or the gobbling up of another people's country. In either case, no win-win situation results.

Regarding Bush II's 40 thieves, we refer primarily to the neocons, who surround him and, in fact, run the shadow government. In the process of furthering their dark agendas, they usurp power, stripping the American people of their rights, natural resources, jobs, respect as a nation, and international admiration. This is thievery of the most severe order.

Neocons advance an arrogant moral authority in doing whatever it takes to further their ominous plans for world domination, regardless the cost of human lives or hard-earned American taxpayer dollars. Beware any thought of opposing them. Bush II made it clear that "you are either with us or against us", meaning that the War on Terrorism is a war between good and evil, with Bush II wearing the tall white hat.

Neocons believe, as some of the 40 thieves testify, that the United States, by virtue of its good nature, warrants its goal of world domination. They are hypocritical in furthering their agenda; one day propping up a dictator if it serves their purposes; the next day, overthrowing him.

Not all of Bush II's thieves serve in his administration. Most of them do. The rest arrive at the White House by various routes. Collectively, they cost America citizens dearly, because their mission of world domination is nothing more than a roundabout way of trading lands and lives for oil.

How did so many thieves penetrate the highest levels of the United States government? To read their official biographies, one would assume they did so by hard work and sheer determination, with a sprinkle of good luck. Not so. Most of them have connections to major corporations that will rake in millions of dollars expanding the US military and fighting the War on Terrorism.

The neocons in the Bush II Administration lied us into war, bankrupted the nation, and made America the second most hated nation on Earth. As Irene Khan, secretary-general of Amnesty International said on May 26, 2004, "Washington's global anti-terror policies are bankrupt of vision and bereft of principle. The world is crying out for principled leadership. Governments are losing their moral compass, sacrificing the global values of human rights in a blind pursuit of security."

43

RICHARD CHENEY

> *Violence is not and cannot exist by itself. It is invariably intertwined with the lie.*
> Alexander Solzhenitsyn, on accepting the Nobel Prize for Literature

The Vice President of the United States is really the President or the ever-present shadow of Bush II, elected by the Supreme Court to be President. In other words, if Bush II is the Puppet President, Cheney is the puppet master. He is also Super Hawk, who wants perpetual war, and he maintains his own national security operation toward that end.

At first glance, Cheney's biography highlights a distinguished career in business and government service. He served four presidents and won elections to the US Congress himself. His official profile, posted on the White House web site, states, "Throughout his service, Mr. Cheney served with duty, honor, and unwavering leadership, gaining him the respect of the American people during trying military times." That refers, no doubt, to Desert Storm, when Cheney was Bush I's Secretary of Defense and co-mastermind of the first Iraq War. Perhaps it referred to another large military operation that he directed — Operation Just Cause in Panama.

Although Cheney's official bio mentions business in passing, in reality his high-ranking positions in the oil industry have managed to amass him a fortune. During his five years as Chairman and CEO of Halliburton — the Texas-based energy company — Cheney sat atop global deals that eventually raised questions in the US Congress and the Securities and Exchange Commission (SEC).

He, like Kenneth Lay at Enron, serves as a clear example of how corporate America has erred in its way of doing business. Secrecy, loopholes, backdoor negotiations and loose accounting practices abound. In the process, Cheney and Lay have become very, very rich. Lay, so far, has skated on all charges in his tanking of Enron, which cost its employees millions of dollars in lost wages and pensions.

In 2003, as in every year since Cheney left Halliburton, he pocketed more than $175,000 in deferred pay as a part of a departure deal he struck with the company. That was aside from the $36 million payoff for his final year at the company's helm.

Investigation of his dealings at Halliburton and subsequent energy meetings after he became Vice President are still underway. The conflict-of-interest case, which has been placed before the US Supreme Court, continues to draw fire, especially at times when US Justice Antonio Scalia goes hunting with Cheney, hinting at impropriety, at least. Will the American public ever know who participated in secret meetings that set the US energy agenda? Not if Cheney has anything to say about it.

When Cheney was Bush I's Secretary of Defense, he reversed the rules that prevented private contractors from working on US military bases, thereby opening doors for companies like Kellogg Brown & Root, a subsidiary of Halliburton, to receive billions in contracts. When he became CEO of Halliburton, he recruited his military aide at the Pentagon to become senior vice president in charge of Pentagon dealings. Talk about slick.

The pattern he set continued long after he left Halliburton and resumed public service. The company has been the main beneficiary of the rush by the Pentagon to build anti-terrorism military bases around the world, costing the taxpayers billions upon billions of dollars. Without any cost controls, the tab would be significantly greater than if the military did their own construction work. Someone facilitated those contracts, although Cheney denies any impropriety. TIME magazine, however, in its June 4, 2004 issue, offers proof from the Pentagon of Cheney's complicity in Halliburton's contracts.

As CEO, Cheney did not provide Halliburton with stellar leadership. In fact, the company fell short of expectations on Wall Street more than once; that is, until the company changed its accounting procedures.

Under Cheney's direction, Halliburton inflated profits by more than $200 million over a four-year period, largely by assuming it could collect on cost overruns on its large number of construction projects. Not until a year later did the company report its accounting tricks to the SEC or to Halliburton investors. More than a dozen lawsuits resulted, including one by Judicial Watch.

The accounting firm behind the shenanigans was Arthur Andersen, convicted in 2002 of obstruction of justice for shredding Enron documents. In 1996, Cheney, who seemed to admire Arthur Andersen's accounting practices, endorsed the firm in a video.

During Cheney's reign at Halliburton, two of its subsidiaries had contracts with Iraq, although on the 2000 presidential campaign trail, Cheney denied knowledge of any such trading activities. The subsidiaries maintained their trade arrangements for more than a year under Cheney's watch. It seems highly unlikely that he did not know they existed.

When the Supreme Court gave George Bush II the presidency, neocons were relieved that Cheney, one of their highest-ranking members, answered the call to handle the transition. He handpicked the best of the best — but maybe not the brightest, as history might someday judge — in neocon circles, building an administration of ideologues, like-minded in their mission for New World Order. Cheney and these cronies were ready to hit the ground running in the new administration, for they had laid plans years earlier to begin the march toward world conquest and domination.

In 1990, then-Secretary of Defense Cheney quietly commissioned a new strategic plan. Paul Wolfowitz, then Undersecretary for Defense Policy, I. Lewis Libby (now Cheney's chief of staff), and Eric Edelman (Cheney's former senior foreign policy advisor) outlined a policy of US global domination.

In 1997, a group of true believers in the New World Order, led by Cheney, Libby, Wolfowitz, Perle, Rumsfeld, among others, founded the Project for the New American Century (PNAC). which issued a statement of principles that called for an aggressive American policy toward global domination. Jeb Bush also belongs to PNAC. This group forged an alliance with George W. Bush.

Two months before the presidential election of 2000, PNAC issued a position paper, "Rebuilding America's Defenses — Strategy, Forces and Resources for a New Century" — that spelled out the particulars for a global empire strategy. Their four-point plan was to: (1) repudiate the Anti-Ballistic Missile Treaty, (2) build a global missile defense system, and (3) increase defense spending by $20 billion a year to 3.8% of the gross domestic product, and (4) re-invent the US military to meet the expanded obligations around the world.

Cheney and a small group of neocons masterminded the case for the pre-emptive invasion of Iraq as early as 1997, almost four years before 9/11 and three years before Bush II took office. The Cheney-Rumsfeld-Rice trio eventually directed the attack on Iraq and the regime change that resulted. However, not until after Cheney became mesmerized by Ahmad Chalabi, an absolute fraud, who sold the neocons a bill of goods and became quite wealthy in the process.

A few years ago, Congress handed Chalabi's group $94 million of the taxpayers' money. Throughout the war and its aftermath, the US paid Chalabi's Iraq National Congress a monthly stipend of $340,000, until he fell out of favor recently, much to the embarrassment of the neocons.

Chalabi gave the neocons everything they wanted to hear — from Arabs dancing in the street after 9/11 to Saddam's weapons of mass destruction and other inaccurate intelligence. All of his stories were lies. Those lies served as the basis for Cheney's pitch to Bush that the United States should go to war.

In the months that followed 9/11, Cheney carried out the duties of running the country from a variety of hiding places, including his Beltway Bunker, rarely surfacing for an interview. He has been the power behind the Bush II throne, calling the shots, even down to instructing Bush II on what to say and how to say it in official meetings, at press conferences, and before the general public.

His most obvious propping became evident when Bush II refused to testify before the 9/11 Commission unless Cheney appeared with him. All jokes aside — and there were many — Cheney pulls the strings in this puppet government.

CONDOLEEZZA RICE

We need a common enemy to unite us.
Condoleezza Rice, March 2000

When Condoleezza Rice became Bush II's National Security Advisor to Bush II, one of her first duties was to rewrite the job description of her position. Instead of including weightier responsibilities one might expect of a National Security Advisor, Rice's role principally involves making her boss look good. That is a tall order when, for example, he asks the President of Brazil if any blacks live there. Rice corrected the embarrassing mistake.

So it has been with whatever the crisis at hand requires. Rice steps in and polishes the presidential image, imparts important information as Bush needs it, and helps him pronounce the names of visiting heads of state to avoid further national embarrassment.

Rice's experience in the oil industry, though limited to a directorship at Chevron-Texaco, made her one of the boys in Bush II's Administration. Chevron even named its largest oil tanker after her, although later changed it, most likely due to excessive public attention that proved embarrassing to Bush.

Rice worked for the Reagan Administration and later the Bush I Administration. By then, she had become quite an expert on the Soviet Union, which no longer exists.

Rice served on other boards of directors - Transamerica, Hewlett Packard, Charles Schwab and The Rand Corporation. In 1993, Stanford University appointed her provost, which she maintained until 1999, when Bush II tapped her to help with his presidential campaign. In 2001, Bush II appointed her National Security Advisor.

As National Security Advisor, she participates in the Administration's lies, deception and cover-up regarding the Oil War II, the War on Terrorism, and just about everything else Bush and his thieves do. Many of the lies were unmasked, followed by Administration denials rather than admissions of guilt. Rice's lies include committing perjury before the 9/11 Commission.

Before the Commission, Rice demonstrated her incompetence by referring to the 1983 truck bombing of the US Marine barracks in Beirut a terrorist act. In fact, the bombing took place in retaliation of our shelling a Muslim village near Beirut by the USS New Jersey a month earlier.

Despite overwhelming evidence to the contrary, Rice insisted that no one could have predicted the use of airplanes to attack buildings like the World Trade Center and the Pentagon. Despite overwhelming evidence to the contrary, she insisted that Saddam Hussein had weapons of mass destruction. Despite overwhelming evidence to the contrary, Rice publicly stated that the

Bush II Administration never connected Saddam Hussein to al-Qaeda or 9/11.

In addition, Rice maintained a peaceful front for Bush's cronies, who relentlessly advanced their plans for war, insisting that the Administration preferred a peaceful, diplomatic solution to war. She said words to that effect as late as March 2003, long after the inner circle decided to launch a pre-emptive war against Iraq. After all, her job is to make the President look good, even if means stretching the truth.

Being the highest-ranking black woman in US government, one would think she would have the full support of the African-American constituency. Not so. When Rice stood dutifully by Bush II as he declared the University of Michigan Law School's affirmative action program unconstitutional, blacks for whom affirmative action holds a high position on their national agenda considered it treasonous. Some blacks have called her a race traitor, others the devil's handmaiden for willingly serving the most dangerous president in modern US history.

How history will judge Rice, also known as the "Warrior Princess", is uncertain, but it could be unfavorable, at least. After all, as more and more evidence reveals that the US waged Oil War II out of greed and sloppy intelligence, her tooting the horn of national security falls on deaf ears.

Add to that her own lies and attempts to cover up the prisoner abuse in Iraq, and it becomes more apparent that history may not be kind to Rice. Although the Red Cross contacted Rice in January 2004 about the abuses, on March 19, 2004, on the CBS "Early Show", she remarked, "There are no more rape rooms and torture chambers in Iraq." Clearly, she lied.

Former President Al Gore recently called for her resignation. "Condoleezza Rice, who has badly mishandled the coordination of national security policy, should resign immediately."

PAUL WOLFOWITZ

The nature of power attracts the very sort of people who should not have it.
Mike Rivero, whatreallyhappened.com

Although Paul Wolfowitz serves as Bush II's Deputy Defense Secretary, some believe he would have Rumsfeld's job if his views were not those of an extremist. He is truly the Defense mastermind of the Bush II Administration. He also serves as Bush II's Jewish foreign policy campaign advisor.

One of the most hawkish pro-Israel neocons, he is a leading supporter of Ariel Sharon and his dark agenda for domination in the Middle East. Wolfowitz maintains close ties to the Israeli military and has family living in Israel. He was one of the driving forces behind Oil War II in Iraq.

From 1989 to 1993, Wolfowitz served as Undersecretary of Defense for Policy in charge of a 700-member team that assumed a major responsibility for reshaping military strategy and policy at the end of the Cold War. He co-wrote with Lewis Libby the 1992 draft "Defense Planning Guidance", calling for US military dominance over Eurasia and pre-emptive strikes against countries suspected of developing weapons of mass destruction. Except Israel. After it leaked to *The New York Times*, the draft set off so many alarms that they had to rewrite it substantially.

One of Wolfowitz's strategic plans for the Middle East involves (1) pushing the Palestinians from the West Bank into Jordan, (2) renaming Jordan Palestine, (3) removing the Jordanian monarchy to head a US-backed new regime in Iraq (enabling the US to control access to Iraq oil), and (4) revenging Saudi Arabia for its support of Islamic fundamentalism.

After 9/11, many of the principles of that draft became policy points in the 2002 National Security Strategy of the United States. During the 1991 Gulf War, Wolfowitz advocated extending the war's aim to include toppling Saddam Hussein's regime. He, Cheney and Rumsfeld considered Saddam "unfinished business" from the first Iraq War.

On September 14, 2001, Wolfowitz declared at a press conference that the US government was committed to "ending states that sponsor terrorism." That was a public rebuke of Powell, who had consistently resisted PNAC's aggressive positions regarding world domination.

In October 2002, Wolfowitz asserted, "This fight is a broad fight. It's a global fight. The war on terrorism is a global war, and one that must be pursued everywhere." He singled out Jordan, Pakistan and Yemen as his high-priority targets in the fight against terrorism. These targets were at odds with Bush's "Axis of Evil" — Iraq, Iran and North Korea.

In April 2003, Wolfowitz became the first in the Bush II Administration to call for action against Syria for harboring Iraqi leaders and weapons of mass destruction as the US launched its invasion. "There's got to be a change in Syria," he said, accusing President Bashar Assad of "extreme ruthlessness".

RICHARD PERLE

It is my conviction that killing under the cloak of war is nothing but an act of murder.
Albert Einstein

Dubbed the Prince of Darkness for his hard-line posture on national security issues, Richard Perle was the Foreign Policy Advisor to Secretary of Defense Donald Rumsfeld until March 2003. He resigned from the chairmanship of the Defense Policy Board at the Pentagon over conflict of interest issues. There is every reason to believe that Perle still contributes his advice about national foreign policy. After all, he is just a telephone call away.

One of the main planners of Oil War II, Perle is a master of the language of force, murder and destruction. In his book, *An End to Evil*, he called for support for Israel to impose its unchallenged supremacy in the Middle East, claiming that Arabs are not psychologically fit to reconcile themselves with today's world.

Perle was the chief architect of the "creative destruction agenda" to reshape the Middle East, starting with the invasion of Iraq. He outlined parts of this agenda in a key 1996 report for Israel's right-wing Likud Party, called, "A Clean Break: A New Strategy for Securing the Realm." Hey, which country's taxpayers are paying this guy, anyway?

Perle helped establish two think tanks — the Center for Security Policy and the Jewish Institute for National Security (JINSA). He is a fellow at the American Enterprise Institute and an advisor for the counter-terrorist think tank, Foundation for the Defense of Democracies. He is also a director of *The Jerusalem Post*. Perle also runs Hollinger Digital, part of the group that publishes *The Daily Telegram* in Great Britain.

Many believe he is an Israeli government agent. He lost his job in the office of US Senator Henry "Scoop" Jackson in the 1970s after the National Security Agency caught him passing highly classified documents to the Israeli Embassy. When Jonathan Pollard did the same thing, he went to prison.

In Paul Findley's book, *They Dare to Speak Out*, he wrote, "An FBI summary of a 1970 wiretap recorded Perle discussing classified information with someone at the Israeli Embassy. He came under fire in 1983 when newspapers reported he received substantial payments to represent the interests of an Israeli weapons company [Soltam]. Perle denied conflict of interest, insisting that, although he received payment for these services after he had assumed his position in the Defense Department, he was between jobs when he worked for the Israeli firm."

Perle is a member of the JINSA Board of Advisors. He is one of the leading supporters of Ariel Sharon and one of the most high profile neocons in the country today. He was one of 31 people who signed a letter to President Bush II, urging regime change in Iraq and increased support of Israel.

I. LEWIS LIBBY

If Richard Cheney is the most powerful man in America, his Chief of Staff and National Security Advisor, I. Lewis "Scooter" Libby, owns his share of power, too. He is Cheney's chief pro-Israel Jewish advisor, which helps explain why Cheney was so eager to wage war with Iraq again. The United States engaged in that war, not to oust Saddam or secure Iraq's oil, but primarily for Israel. Libby has longstanding ties to Ariel Sharon.

Libby was the attorney for Mark Rich, convicted felon and Israeli spy, whom President Clinton pardoned within days of leaving office. The US Department of Justice indicted Rich in 1983 on the felony charges of tax evasion and trading with the enemy.

A protege of Wolfowitz for more than 30 years, Libby assembled the "shadow National Security Council" in Cheney's office that protects the Israeli agents inside the Pentagon and State Department.

He is part of the inner circle of neocons that pushed for war with Iraq before Bush became President. Libby and Cheney trumped up a number of lies to build a case for Oil War II, including the alleged connection between Saddam Hussein and Mohamed Atta, the alleged chief hijacker on 9/11.

As Bush I's Principal Deputy Undersecretary of Defense and later Deputy Undersecretary of Defense for Policy, Libby secured a reputation as a leading neocon ideologist.

He is a founding member of PNAC. In 2000, he joined Wolfowitz, William Kristol, Robert Kagan and others in writing "Rebuilding America's Defenses — Strategy, Forces and Resources for a New Century," a report that he and Wolfowitz originally presented to Cheney in 1992.

That original draft argued that the US should use pre-emptive force to prevent countries from developing weapons of mass destruction, acting alone, if necessary. Someone leaked it to *The New York Times*, abruptly arresting its use then. Later, the pre-emptive ideas became part of Bush II's national security strategy. They served as the basis of the founding principles of PNAC, which includes fellow hawkish luminaries as Cheney, Wolfowitz, and Rumsfeld.

It is a draw between Libby and Karl Rove as to which one leaked the identity of CIA agent, Valerie Plame (wife of former Ambassador Joseph Wilson) to newsman Robert Novak. The offense is a felony. Whoever is responsible should be imprisoned.

DONALD RUMSFELD

I am fed up to my ears of old men dreaming of wars for young men to die in.
George McGovern

When George W. Bush appointed Donald Rumsfeld his Secretary of Defense, the American public inherited a big problem. Rumsfeld, with a history of narrow-minded combative management syndrome, may not have been the right one to oversee the US military.

The architect of the Iraq War, Rumsfeld saw his masterpiece fall apart. In fact, Oil War II might qualify as the worst blunder in US military history. In the process, he sparked hatred between civilian and military factions in the Defense Department and created serious morale problems in the troops serving in Iraq.

Rumsfeld's battle plan was shortsighted. It underestimated the number of troops needed to overthrow the Saddam Hussein regime, secure the country and carry out reconstruction. He had no exit plan, and both current and former military generals openly criticized him for that. He snubbed military advisors who knew better how to wage a war and prevail.

Rumsfeld often referred to anyone fighting the US military in Iraq as "thugs", "hoodlums" and worse, conditioning the troops to regard their prisoners as subhuman.

That Rumsfeld developed a master plan to overthrow Saddam Hussein demonstrated the hypocrisy of this Administration. In 1983, when Rumsfeld served as Reagan's special envoy, he glad-handed Saddam on behalf of Bechtel to secure a contract for building an oil pipeline from Iraq to Jordan. Pictures show Rumsfeld cordially shaking Saddam's hand, although the deal never materialized. The second time Rumsfeld met with Saddam was the same day that a UN team confirmed Saddam gassed Iranian troops. That did not stop the Reagan Administration — or Rumsfeld — from diplomacy-for-profit games with the Iraqi dictator.

When it came time to oust Saddam, the Pentagon manipulated documents that Saddam sent to the UN to prove that he did not have weapons of mass destruction. The Pentagon scrutinized tens of thousands of pages, and inappropriately deleted 11,800 of them before forwarding Saddam's dossier to the United Nations. We may never know what those pages contained, but Saddam listed companies that originally supplied him with weapons of mass destruction, including some in the United States. As the joke back then went, "How do we know Iraq has weapons of mass destruction? We have the receipts."

Throughout wars and rumors of war, Rumsfeld has handled questions from the media with disdain. We have yet to know how skillful Rumsfeld is at handling the press, for, as respected White House journalist Helen Thomas once said, "The press is in a coma."

While Rumsfeld calls for expanding the War on Terrorism, other nations keep popping up in the news as potential targets. The current state of affairs, however, suggests that the United States is in no position to impose our homegrown values on any other nation, let alone Iraq. Considering that this nation faces a $500 billion deficit and already stretches thin its army of 480,000, it is impossible to consider waging wars around the world.

The moral responsibility for the scandalous, dismal failure in Iraq rises to the top of the Department of Defense, to the criminal mastermind of the Iraq War himself. Bush stands by him, and praises his civilian and military components in the Defense Department.

Many have called for Rumsfeld's resignation, along with that of Wolfowitz, Feith and Cambone. Former Vice President Al Gore, joined the growing forces demanding their resignation. "The nation is especially at risk every single day that Rumsfeld runs the Secretary of Defense."

As if the ship could not sink deeper, everyone on board continues to participate in a massive cover-up campaign, preferring to lay blame at the feet of a few wayward young soldiers.

"What's most terrifying about this is the argument that the administration has been making since 9/11 — that the president has unlimited power to do whatever he deems necessary," said Avi Cover, a senior attorney with the US Law and Security program of Human Rights First, formerly known as Lawyers Committee for Human Rights. "It doesn't matter what Congress says, what the constitution says, or what international law says."

If the same rules apply to us that we have advocated in international tribunals on Yugoslavia and Rwanda (that civilian leadership is responsible for war crimes committed by their militaries), notes Scott Horton, president of the International League for Human Rights and an expert on military law, "then Donald Rumsfeld is in very serious trouble."

DOUGLAS FEITH

Douglas Feith, a pro-Israel extremist, currently serves as Undersecretary of Defense and Policy Advisor at the Pentagon. As one who considers Richard Perle his mentor, he consistently advocates anti-Arab policies.

An attorney, Feith runs a small law firm, Feith & Zell, with only one international office — in Israel. Most of their legal work represents Israeli interests, particularly that nation's war machine. His partner, L. Marc Zell, represents the Jewish settlers' movement on the West Bank. Feith's own web site, before he accepted his current government post, stated that he "represents Israeli armaments manufacturer."

Feith, a protégé of Richard Perle and former chairman of Rumsfeld's Defense Policy Board, is in the middle of Washington's neocons that support Israel. He was against the Oslo Accord and Camp David peace agreement brought about by former President Jimmy Carter.

Feith's office collected data from Iraqi exiles and scoured other raw intelligence for useful information to make a case for pre-emptive war. He is one of the leading supporters of Ariel Sharon in the Bush II Administration.

As the Number Three civilian member at the Pentagon, after Rumsfeld and Wolfowitz, he served the Reagan Administration as Deputy Assistant Secretary of Defense for Negotiations Policy. Before that, he worked as special counsel to Richard Perle. From 1981-82, he served as a Middle East specialist for the National Security Council, and in 1989, as a lobbyist for the Turkish government, he worked with Perle to build military ties between Turkey and Israel.

Feith follows his mentor's lead in opposing the 1972 Anti-Ballistic Missile Treaty and the Chemical and Biological Weapons conventions, and in supporting the Likud, the settlement movement in the occupied territories, and in stirring support of the Christian Right.

Feith's support of Ariel Sharon's Likud Party has brought him appreciation and recognition. In 1997, he and his father, Dalck Feith, a formerly active Zionist in his native Poland, received recognition for their "service to Israel and the Jewish people" by the pro-Likud Zionist Organization of America (ZOA) at their 100th Anniversary banquet.

Feith remains closely linked to the ZOA, often speaking at their conferences. That group attacks even Jews who do not agree with its extremist views. In 1992, he served with Perle on the Advisory Board for JINSA, which promotes military ties between the US and Israel. He is former chairman and current director of the Center for Security Policy.

In "A Strategy for Israel", an article he wrote in 1997, Feith argued that Israel should renounce the Oslo accords and reoccupy those parts of the West Bank and Gaza that had been transferred to the Palestinian Authority.

In 1999, Feith and Perle again teamed up in their appeal to President Clinton to work with Ahmed Chalabi's Iraq National Congress (INC) to effect regime change. The following year, they endorsed a call for the United States to prepare for a military attack against Syria if its government did not withdraw troops from Lebanon.

As Feith's credibility rapidly evaporates, he could be next in line to lose his job. The mistakes surrounding that pre-emptive strike trace directly back to Feith, who gathered (false) intelligence with the help of Chalabi to prepare an alarmist anti-Saddam case that he handed to Cheney and Rumsfeld.

His office carried the responsibility of post-war planning, but in the process ignored wise counsel that predicted many of the problems that have surfaced since Bush II declared the end of the war. Feith and the Coalition Provisional Authority (CPA) doled out enormous no-bid contracts to corporations that support the Bush Administration, including Halliburton and Bechtel.

STEPHEN CAMBONE

The problem in Defense is how far you go [in military spending] without destroying from within what you are trying to defend from without.
President Dwight D. Eisenhower

That Stephen Cambone carries the title of Donald Rumsfeld's henchman is not surprising to those who know his history. He and Rumsfeld go back years, when Rumsfeld served in Congress and chaired two congressional commissions, one on missile defense and the other on space weapons. Cambone, outspoken about missile defense systems, served as staff director on both commissions.

Wolfowitz, R. James Woolsey (two other thieves in this tragedy), and others served on Rumsfeld's commissions. The result became the blueprint for Bush II's defense policies.

Shortly after Rumsfeld became Bush II's Secretary of Defense, he made Cambone his special assistant. Then, in 2003, Rumsfeld prevailed upon Congress to allow him to create a new senior-level position in the Pentagon — the Undersecretary of Defense for Intelligence. He had a secret motive in doing so: the consolidation of Defense intelligence programs so as to undermine the CIA and former Director George Tenet. No love lost there. Cambone's deputy for operations is none other than the Bible-thumping, anti-Muslim Lt. General William Boykin.

As Rumsfeld's right-hand man, Cambone has few friends in the Pentagon. Both military and civilians there despise him and fear him. That was before he joined the Bush II Administration. Now, they — and the CIA — have even more reason to hate him. He was one of the staunchest believers that Iraq had weapons of mass destruction.

In a 2001 issue of *The Washington Monthly*, the following comments speak to the hatred of Rumsfeld and Cambone. *It would be hard to exaggerate how much Secretary of Defense Donald Rumsfeld and his top aide Stephen Cambone were hated within the Pentagon prior to 9/11. Among other things, Rumsfeld and Cambone foolishly excluded top civilian and military leaders when planning an overhaul of the military to meet new threats, thereby ensuring even greater bureaucratic resistance.*

According to *The Washington Post*, an Army general joked that 'if he had one round left in his revolver, he would take out Stephen Cambone.'

Cambone vigorously defended Rumsfeld and Feith at the recent congressional hearing on Iraqi prisoner abuse. He differed with Major General Antonio Taguba, who first investigated the prisoner abuse at Abu Ghraib Prison in Iraq. Cambone's office, according to the May 12, 2004 edition of

The Washington Post, approved the interrogation practices that are in direct violation of the Geneva Conventions.

Cambone played word games on whether the Geneva Conventions applied to intelligence gathering in Iraq. White House legal counsel, Alberto Gonzales, wrote a memo to Bush II that addressed that point and might have served as the legal foundation for abuse of Iraqi prisoners.

According to the May 24, 2004 issue of *Newsweek*, within months of the 9/11 attacks, Gonzales wrote, "As you have said, the war on terrorism is a new kind of war. In my judgment, this new paradigm renders obsolete Geneva's strict limitations on questioning of enemy prisoners and renders quaint some of its provisions."

Newsweek noted that Secretary of State Colin Powell "hit the roof" when he saw Gonzales's memo. He warned Bush II that any new rules that do not comply with the Geneva Conventions "will reverse over a century of US policy and practice" and have a "high cost in terms of negative international reaction."

By January 25, 2002, Bush II had already decided that the Geneva Conventions did not apply to the questioning of Taliban or al-Qaeda prisoners. Bush II, Rumsfeld and Attorney General John Ashcroft all signed off on a memo on a secret system of detention and interrogation that opened the gate for prisoner abuses in Iraq. Now Ashcroft faces Contempt of Congress charges for not releasing the "smoking gun", the entire memo authorizing torture that points directly at George W. Bush.

Cambone insists that Rumsfeld and General Myers approved the interrogation tactics and that he, Cambone, delivered the approved orders to Abu Ghraib Prison.

One additional note: Before joining the Bush II Administration, Cambone worked for SRS Technologies, a defense contractor that recently secured a $6 million contract to provide administrative and management support for the Missile Defense Agency. Another fat cat gets fatter under Bush II.

JOHN ASHCROFT

Power always has to be kept in check; power exercised in secret, especially under the cloak of national security, is doubly dangerous.
Senator William Proxmire

When John Ashcroft took office as the United States Attorney General, someone handed him a pair of scissors and a copy of the Bill of Rights, the Declaration of Independence, and the US Constitution. Nothing as been the same ever since.

Bush II thinks he picked the best man to be his Attorney General, calling him a "man of great integrity, a man of great judgment, and a man who knows the law." Like the neocon warmongers, 9/11 gave Ashcroft license to steal, and steal, he did, all in the red, white and blue wrappings of patriotism and protection from evil doers.

While the Bush II Administration eagerly promoted their idea of delivering democracy to Afghanistan and Iraq, Ashcroft was busy taking away ours. The Patriot Act breezed through the US Congress and Senate, granting Ashcroft virtually unlimited powers to rescind rights, snoop and spy, selectively slam doors shut on immigrants, conduct racial profiling, and imprison individuals indefinitely without cause.

"Since Jesus, Moses and Abraham (peace be upon them) were not European, would they be escorted off planes if alive today?" asks Imam Abdul Malik.

Justice turned into injustice. Truth turned into lies. Democracy turned into deception. Ashcroft pulled it off boldly. In a few months, he transformed a great democracy into a semi-police state.

We could write a book about John Ashcroft's destruction of civil liberties in the United States. Sometimes, brevity serves best. The people reject Patriot Act I and II, as witnessed by hundreds of communities enacting resolutions to uphold civil rights and civil liberties and demanding that the Constitution be upheld for the protection of all citizens.

It behooves all of Americans to become vigilant, not out of suspicion that a neighbor might be a terrorist, but that one day we will wake up and find ourselves living the nightmare of fascism. Regarding Ashcroft's America, Ayn Rand summed it up in *Atlas Shrugged*: *There is no way to rule innocent people. The only power any government has is the power to crack down on criminals. Well, when there aren't enough criminals, one makes them. One declares so many things to be a crime that it becomes impossible for men to live without breaking the law.*

If there is any doubt that the Bush Administration poses a greater threat to liberty as we know it than al-Qaeda, Attorney General John Ashcroft dispels that doubt regularly. He defends warrantless searches, imprisonment without due process, secret tribunals, and eavesdropping on defense lawyers. He end-runs state laws by federal edict. He scorns federal law by ordering his staff to comply as minimally as possible or not at all with such open-government tools as the Freedom of Information Act. He subordinates the Constitution to religious beliefs. When challenged, he attacks his critics for brandishing "phantoms of lost liberties."

Ashcroft's latest problem surrounds the leaked Pentagon memo dealing with authorization of torture. That memo, which Ashcroft refuses to hand over in its entirety to Congress, and other documents like it attempt to justify illegal acts of murder, theft and torture. This goes back to one of the basic rules of war described by Sun Tzu, that the warring people must be made to believe that they have the moral law on their side. In the current war, justification for the use of torture lays in the claim that the enemy subjected to it was special and unique, that they were terrorists in league with al-Qaeda.

KARL ROVE

Most propaganda is designed not to fool the critical thinker but only to give mortal cowards an excuse not to think at all.
Michael Rivero, whatreallyhappened.com

In the puppet presidency, when puppeteer Cheney is unavailable to pull the strings, Karl Rove steps in and takes over. In a shadowy White House, Rove casts an ever-present shadow around Bush II. Like a good dog trainer, when Rove says, "Sic 'em", Bush launches a war.

Rove runs the domestic policy operation in the White House, as such, being largely responsible for staging the Iraq War to its political advantage. As master of disinformation, he choreographed the Iraq War to coincide with the 2002 mid-term elections, to boost the GOP chances in congressional races. To launch the war "on schedule", he convinced Bush II to connect the dots between Saddam Hussein and Osama bin Laden, even if the CIA could not do it. His plan worked. During the war, a Pew Survey showed that 61% of Americans believed that the two (Hussein and bin Laden) were complicit in the 9/11 attacks.

One day, if former Ambassador Joseph Wilson has his fondest wish granted, he will witness the law enforcement officers handcuffing Rove and leading him out of the White House. The reason: Rove's complicity in exposing Wilson's wife, Valerie Plame, as a CIA undercover agent and endangering her life.

Rove ran dirty political tricks operations as far back as 1972 when Nixon ran for the presidency. He learned the art of dirty tricks from the master, Donald Segretti (of the old Nixon days). Rove hit his stride by dirtying up the John McCain campaign in 2000, spreading lies and casting aspersions on him personally and on his family.

Other politicians who have come under the chicanery of Segretti and Rove were Ed Muskie, George McGovern, Jimmy Carter, Walter Mondale, Al Gore, Robert Dole, Ross Perot, and whoever else threatened their candidate. He was also complicit in the campaign to unseat former Congresswoman Cynthia McKinney, who was the first nationally known politician to question Bush's foreknowledge of 9/11.

MICHAEL LEDEEN

In the US today, the Declaration of Independence hangs on schoolroom walls, but foreign policy follows Machiavelli.
Howard Zinn

As if Karl Rove could not come up with enough sinister plans himself, he has Michael Ledeen, one of the most radical neocons frequently advising him — and Bush II — on foreign policy matters. Unlike others in the inner neocon circle, Ledeen rarely faces public scrutiny, most likely because his views are not palatable for even the most conservative public. Nevertheless, Ledeen carries considerable weight in US foreign policy matters in the Middle East.

Ledeen remains one of the most vocal supporters for regime change in Iran. That's right. Iran. In 2001, he co-founded the Coalition for Democracy in Iran. He quickly saw past Iraq to other targets in the region.

A resident scholar at the American Enterprise Institute, he works closely with Richard Perle, making an extremist pro-Israel pair. Some consider Ledeen one of the meanest fascists to surface since the end of World War II, who supports regime change through the Middle East — Iran, Iraq, Syria and Saudi Arabia.

Ledeen served with Secretary of Defense Alexander Haig in the Reagan Administration. He also served in the State Department and National Security Council. He wrote *The War against the Terror Masters*, advocating regime change in Iran, Syria and Saudi Arabia.

He is a member of the JINSA Advisory Board and one of its founding organizers. In April 2003, he delivered an address for JINSA's policy forum. In the speech, entitled "Time to Focus on Iran — The Mother of Modern Terrorism", he said that the "time for diplomacy is at an end; it is time for a free Iran, free Syria and free Lebanon." He believes the responsibility for distributing all this democracy rests on America's manifest destiny and that the change will come through a violent "total war."

In a summary of his book, *The War against the Terror Masters*, he writes, "We wage total war because we fight in the name of an idea, and ideas either triumph or fail, totally."

To Ledeen, the only strategy America can use is force to instill its ideology on its enemies. He states, in an example of Machiavellian inspiration, "We can lead by the force of high moral example, [but] fear is much more reliable, and lasts longer. Once we show that we are capable of dealing out terrible punishment to our enemies, our power will be far greater."

Ledeen regularly takes issue with the more dove-like State Department and the diplomatic United Nations. He also berates the CIA for hedging on revealing evidence — true or false — which would justify military action. It is too soon to know if the United States will heed Ledeen's advice about attacking Iran, Syria and Lebanon, but his past influence bears noting. He preached for regime change in Iraq for years, and realized his dream when the US launched its pre-emptive illegal war there.

It also bears noting that Ledeen was highly influential in disenfranchising the State Department and CIA from decisions about Iraq. Perhaps in his eagerness to shut them out, he opened doors to the mess we now face in Iraq.

DAVID WURMSER

Another leading supporter of Ariel Sharon in the Bush II Administration, David Wurmser works for Libby in Cheney's office. A neocon, close friend of Perle and Likud mole, Wurmser enjoys belonging to the inner circle of neocons, which dominates US foreign policy and national security in the Bush II Administration.

Wurmser once served as a special assistant to John R. Bolton at the State Department and was a research fellow on the Middle East at the American Enterprise Institute. He was the principle author of a 1996 report by a task forced headed by Perle, called the "Study Group on a New Israeli Strategy toward 2000." The report, directed to incoming Israeli Prime Minister Binyamin Netanyahu, recommended that Israel end the process of trading land for peace. Instead, it promoted changing the balance of power in the Middle East by forming an axis of Israel, Turkey and Jordan.

Wurmser supported the joint Israel-US defeat of Iraq and advocated overthrowing the Saddam Hussein regime. In 1997, he wrote a column in the Wall Street Journal called 'Iraq Needs a Revolution.' A year later, he and Perle signed a letter calling for full US support of the Iraqi National Congress (INC), led by the crook, Ahmad Chalabi. He also promoted the notion of an alliance between Jordan and the INC to redraw the Middle East. Ironically, Chalabi faces felony charges in Jordan that could put him in prison for a long time.

Wurmser has long called for a joint US-Israel effort to topple the Syrian government. During the latter part of the 1990s, he wrote frequently in support of destroying the regime of then-President Hafez Assad. By so doing, he figured, it would speed the creation of a new order in Lebanon dominated by "tribal, familial, and clan unions under limited governments."

Wurmser and his fellow neocons, who fell for Chalabi's con, used his false intelligence as a basis for the US pre-emptive illegal war in Iraq. In the process of covering their lies and deception, they stole American taxpayer dollars and wasted the lives of young American troops.

COLIN L. POWELL

I want to scare the hell out of the rest of the world.
General Colin Powell on US military power prior to the 1991 Gulf War

United States Secretary of State for Bush II, Colin Powell was Joint Chiefs of Staff, the highest-ranking military position in the Department of Defense, under Bush I. During that term, from 1989 to 1993, he served as overseer of 28 crises, including Oil War I, or Operation Desert Storm. His nickname, General My Lai, dates back to a much earlier war.

Thirty-six years ago, 500 Vietnamese civilians died in the My Lai massacre, which Powell attempted to cover up. [Seymour Hersch of *The New Yorker* exposed that massacre, just as he exposed the recent Abu Ghraib prison scandal in Iraq.] Comparing US military action in My Lai with ops in Iraq, US actions resulted in more than 10,000 Iraqi civilian deaths in Oil War II, according to Amnesty International and other human rights organizations.

As William Rivers Pitt, editor of truthout.org, so aptly said, "My Lai is the standard by which modern American war atrocities are measured. What is happening in Iraq eclipses My Lai by orders of magnitude."

Powell's crimes as a military officer also include facilitation of US missile sale to Israel, and the massacre of thousands of Panamanian civilians in "Operation Just Cause." He ignored the pleas of Gulf War veterans suffering from Gulf War Syndrome and went before the United Nations to claim with absolute certainty that Iraq possessed weapons of mass destruction. The basis of his claim soon came unraveled. He lied to the United Nations, to the American people and to the world. He later admitted he lied.

Perhaps at the heart of the problem is the fact that Powell, a career military man, serves as Secretary of State. That is like putting a seasoned statesman in charge of the US Army. When Bush appointed Powell Secretary of State, it sent up a red flag that the Administration would force him to comply with a military agenda, rather than follow the path of diplomacy that has been the hallmark of that office.

At times, it seems that Powell wishes he could make good an exit from the Bush II Administration. Perhaps Harry Belafonte touched on the roots of that desire when he said, "There's an old saying in the days of slavery. There are those slaves who lived on the plantation, and there were those slaves who lived in the house. You got the privilege of living in the house if you served the master. Colin Powell was permitted to come into the house of the master."

Therein lies the rub.

RICHARD ARMITAGE

Richard Armitage, known in some Washington circles as "Mr. Cocaine", has deep roots in the production and trafficking of cocaine and heroine on a global scale. Also known as Powell's "Bulldog", he currently serves as the US Deputy Secretary of State — The Number Two position there — and directs the operations of the Foreign Narcotics Control Office. That office helps the CIA in narcotics trafficking to maintain a constant flow of covert revenue through offshore money laundering banks into the legitimate asset portfolios of prominent Americans.

Give Richard Armitage any corner of the world where poppies grow, and an alarming escalation in heroin trafficking will soon occur there. That is interesting, considering his responsibilities include not only containing the growth of drugs but also destruction of crops that make the drugs.

Armitage and people like Elliott Abrams and Frank Carlucci (the Carlyle Group) belong to an interagency group, known as Restricted Access Group One (RAG-1), which formed, managed and controlled the liability of the illegal covert government operation. Shades of Iran-Contra? Allegations indicate Armitage originated the idea of using heroin to weaken the fighting capability of Russian soldiers, who invaded Afghanistan. That was when we were on the other side.

Another scandal involving Armitage concerned the POW/MIAs from the Vietnam War. Lt. Col. Bo Gritz, the most decorated soldier in Vietnam, wrote in his book, *Called to Serve*:

> If Richard Armitage was…a major participant in parallel government drug trafficking, then it explained why our efforts to rescue POWs had been inexplicably foiled, time after time. If it was true, Richard Armitage would be the last man in the world who would desire to see prisoners of war come home alive…Armitage reportedly spent more time repatriating opium profits than recovering POWs. In 1976, when Khun Sa was still selling heroin to CIA officials, the head of the CIA was none other than George Bush (I).
>
> Former presidential candidate H. Ross Perot, appointed presidential investigator for POW/MIA affairs, came upon the same information, and Defense Secretary Frank Carlucci warned him to stop pursuing the connections to Armitage. As [Perot] sadly explained to a group of POW/MIA families in 1987, 'I have been instructed to cease and desist.'

The US military maneuvers in Afghanistan in October 2001 were as much to secure the oil pipelines and poppy fields as they were to capture

Osama bin Laden. Destroying the Taliban meant poppy farmers could return to their fields, and the heroin industry could again flood the world markets.

It did not take long for heroin prices to skyrocket and production to increase from 185 tons in the Taliban days to 3,400 tons in 2002. By then, the US-sponsored puppet government of Hamid Karzai made sure our interests were secure there. In the 18 months after launching attacks on Afghanistan, heroin trafficking in the US grew 380 percent.

The land along the Pakistan and Afghanistan borders, years earlier, became the top producer of heroin in the world and supplied 60 percent of the US demand. The heroin addicts in Pakistan went from almost zero in 1979 to 1.2 million by 1985.

Estimates of $500 billion in revenues generated by CIA-sponsored drug trade in Afghanistan alone are staggering. The CIA — and the US State Department and Pentagon — protects the drug trade through its covert links to organized crime. Revenues come clean through an intricate system of money laundering.

Foreign policy makes strange bedfellows, and in the business of drug trade, it is not odd for friendships to develop where there would otherwise be enemies. After all, drug trafficking is one of the top three most valuable commodities, after oil and arms trade.

Why do some refer to Armitage as "Mr. Cocaine"? It is because he does not limit his operations to poppy fields and heroin trade. Foreign policy — as in the case of Afghanistan — clearly revolves around the US control of drug trade on a global scale.

JOSHUA BOLTEN

The last official act of any government is to loot the nation.
Michael Rivero, whatreallyhappened.com

As Chief Policy Director in the Office of Management and Budget for Bush II, Joshua Bolten oversees the preparation of the federal budget and supervises administration of the budget in agencies within the Executive Branch. When he accepted the appointment, he vowed to be a "tight-fisted custodian of the people's money."

Nicknamed "Switch" by insiders or "The Blade" by Bush II himself, Bolten carries the responsibility of slashing spending and nixing government requests for increased funding. A close look at the outrageously out-of-control spending in less than one term of Bush II shows that Bolten does an equally good job of juggling. He juggles the dollars to suit the whimsical spending habits of Bush II for defense, homeland security, and to secure votes in 2004.

In just three years, Americans have lost billions in aid to education, protection for the environment, benefits for war veterans, assistance for the poor and elderly, and aid to states, leaving many of them near bankruptcy. Even the fiscal conservatives, who once supported Bush's tax cuts for the rich and war spending, no longer tolerate his reckless spending.

Bush — and Bolten — project even more startling budgetary considerations for 2006, presuming Bush is elected (we cannot say re-elected, because he was not elected in 2000). Defense spending would increase by 5.2% and the Justice Department budget would grow by 4.3%, but budgets for education, environmental protection, veteran affairs, and biomedical research would feel the effects of Bolten's slashing. The latter cut is interesting, when Americans face growing threats of bio-terrorism in the United States.

In addition to the increased spending for defense and domestic security, the US budget allows billions for Israel and Bush II's corporate cronies, like Halliburton and Bechtel. Bush's tax cuts for the rich force average Americans to pay a dear price.

A former banker, Bolten joined Bush II campaign in 1999 as policy director. He served as general counsel to the US trade representative and as a White House legislative liaison in the Bush I Administration. In between the two Bush Administrations, he served as a government policy executive with Goldman Sachs in London and as an international trade counsel to the Senate Finance Committee.

As long as we are discussing money and ways that the federal government uses it, here is a lesson that needs heeding. A principle provision of the FEMA [Federal Emergency Management Agency] Executive Orders is that the President — in a financial emergency — can turn off all ATMs and use the cash in the banks as he sees fit to deal with the crisis.

TOM RIDGE

Liberties are not given; they are taken away.
Aldous Huxley

Bush II tapped Tom Ridge, the former governor of Pennsylvania, to be the first Secretary of Homeland Security, a new Cabinet-level post. In that position, Ridge oversees 180,000 employees in a variety of combined agencies. Responsibilities of those agencies include shoring up America's borders, providing intelligence analysis and infrastructure protection, countering the use of weapons of mass destruction through improved uses of science and technology, and producing a comprehensive response and recovery system. Don't forget creating a colorful code to alarm Americans of impending terrorist attacks. Red, Orange, Yellow, whatever.

The former Governor of Pennsylvania may have prepared him for his current position. Known as a law-and-order governor, he mastered the art of getting tough on crime, while enduring considerable controversy in the process. During protests at the 2000 Republican National Convention, Philadelphia resembled a mini-police state. As we said, Ridge was preparing to handle the same authority on a larger scale.

In his first campaign for Governor in 1993, his theme was fighting crime, and soon after he won, he succeeded in getting tough anti-crime laws passed. Later, the courts ruled some of them unconstitutional. Ridge was big on using the police and other law enforcement agencies to carry out his agenda that included the death penalty, trying juveniles as adults and serving in adult prisons, and limiting parole releases. He also imposed fees on prisoners for health care services and drug testing. Echoing Bush II's penchant for state-sponsored executions, Ridge presided over Pennsylvania's first execution since 1960.

Ridge, as Bush II does now, had no tolerance for dissenters, subjecting them to harsh treatment, questionable surveillance tactics, and unwarranted criminal charges, most of which the prosecutors dropped. These practices set him up for the role he plays in helping Attorney General fight the domestic war on terrorism. Anything goes.

STEPHEN J. HADLEY

As Deputy to National Security Advisor Condoleezza Rice, Stephen Hadley made a big mistake that will haunt him for a long time. He apparently forgot to remove the infamous 16-word Niger uranium claim from Bush's State of the Union. Hadley says simply that he was too busy. As it turns out, he represents the ineptitude of people in the Bush II Administration.

We all know the Niger uranium notion landed in the circular file of discredited reasons for going to war with Iraq. That did not stop Hadley from furthering his claim. In the *Chicago Tribune* on February 16, 2003, he wrote:

With its trained nuclear scientists and a weapons design, all Saddam Hussein lacks is the necessary plutonium or enriched uranium. Iraq has an active procurement program. According to British intelligence, the regime has tried to acquire natural uranium from abroad. That statement followed Bush's State of the Union in January.

Hadley finally took the blame, admitting he knew that the Niger uranium claim lacked credibility as early as October 2002. So, why, in February did he make it a case to go to war? It seems that he is what is lacking credibility.

The CIA had warned Hadley twice about the unreliability of the Niger uranium claims in memos dated October 5 and October 6. In both instances, the CIA expressed reservations about the British reporting Iraq's attempts to buy uranium from Niger. Not only did Hadley slip up by not removing the Niger uranium reference from Bush's speech, but he also continued to use it in public commentaries as if he had never heard the claim was worthless.

Stephen Hadley may be the least guilty of the 40 Thieves, but he represents a core problem in the Bush Administration. Those who serve the people of this great land can lie and deceive with impunity, yet those brave souls who have left the Bush II Administration have done so under fire.

ELLIOTT ABRAMS

In December 2002, Elliott Abrams became Special Assistant to Bush II and Senior Director for the National Security Council to direct SW Asia, Near East and North African Affairs. His previous post was Director of the Office for Democracy, Human Rights and International Operations in the National Security Council.

A Zionist extremist, who wrote a book calling for Jews to embrace their faith to curtail assimilation, Abrams maintains a hard line regarding the Israeli-Palestinian conflict. He suggests that Bush II should not encourage Palestinians to perpetuate the myth that they will ever return to claim their former lands in Israel. He is a staunch supporter of Ariel Sharon.

Abrams is one of several criminals (convicted or otherwise) who serve in the Bush II Administration. That Bush — and Reagan — gave him a position to oversee human rights is a travesty with tragic overtones.

As Assistant Secretary of State under President Reagan, Abrams pleaded guilty to two misdemeanors, in both cases lying to Congress over his role in the Iran-Contra affair. He faced felony charges but received one-year probation and 100 hours of community service. A year later, in 1992, Bush I granted him a full pardon.

He was a hawkish pro-Israel member of the Reagan State Department. As Reagan's Assistant Secretary of State for Human Rights and Humanitarian Affairs, Abrams helped cover up a horrible atrocity, a Salvadoran Army massacre in El Mozote that left 800 to 1,000 civilians dead. Along with John Negroponte and Otto Reich, Abrams was complicit in one of the bloodiest scandals in the past 20 years. Hard evidence shows that they aided torturers and death squads, circumvented the US Congress and US Constitution, and deceived the American public.

Abrams was also part of the RAG-1 interagency group, along with Armitage, Carlucci and others, designed to control the Iran-Contra covert operations. He helped found PNAC, along fellow neocons Rumsfeld and Wolfowitz.

He began his political career with US Senator Henry "Scoop" Jackson and held various posts in President Reagan's Administration. He was a senior fellow at the Hudson Institute from 1990-96 before becoming president of the Washington-based "think tank" Ethics and Public Policy Center, which "affirms the political relevance of great western ethical imperatives." He also served as chairman of the US Commission International Religious Freedom.

In 1980, he married Rachel Decter, daughter of neocons, Norman Podhoretz and Midge Decter.

GALE A. NORTON

Gale Norton enjoys hiking in the wilderness with her husband. If she continues serving the demands of corporate America for oil and gas drilling and logging rights in previously protected areas, she might have to settle for walking around Washington, DC instead. From the way she is bent on doling out chunks of America's precious lands and natural resources, one would think Woody Guthrie wrote "This Land Is My Land" just for her.

The United States Secretary of the Interior, charged with overseeing federal decisions about 436 million acres of public land and the country's water management, should be one who loves the outdoors and seeks all ways to preserve our natural resources. In the case of Gale Norton, to assume that, one would be wrong.

When Bush II chose Norton to be is Interior Secretary, the floodgates burst open and corporate lobbyists bent on indiscriminate mining, logging and drilling lined up to be heard. To underscore further the inappropriateness of Bush's choice for Interior Secretary, Norton picked three of the top lobbyists from the energy industry to serve in her department.

Officially, Norton's biography projects her as a conservationist, public servant, and leading advocate of voluntary compliance with environmental rules. The first woman to direct the 156-year-old department, Norton immediately made the 4C's the cornerstone of her office: Consultation, Communication, Cooperation and Conservation. She believes that for conservation to be successful, government must involve people who live and work on the land.

To practice what she believes, she launched ambitions programs that sound good on paper, but she is worse than the notorious James Watts. In fact, some dub her, 'James Watts in a skirt.'

What one does not read in her glowing biography is Norton's record as a lawyer who championed the rights of polluters and corporate interests. These claims alone should have disqualified her from becoming Interior Secretary.

Some of Norton's sins against conservation and wildlife include: Litigating for cattlemen, miners and oil companies, advocating the opening of the Arctic National Wildlife Refuse for oil drilling, and allowing polluters to evade environmental fines. She also advocates undermining the balance between property rights and community interests. One of the more outrageous abuses of her office came when she recently gave the green light for Alaskans to continue the aerial shooting of wolves, despite the fact that Alaskans twice voted against that savage activity.

Not only should Norton enforce stewardship of America's natural resources, public lands and precious wildlife, she also should set the example of stewardship. It is apparent that she does not understand the concept.

GENERAL TOMMY FRANKS

Former top military commander of Iraq War II, who led the invasion, General Tommy Franks retired mid-field, leaving the troops to fight the war without him. For his part in that war, he faces a lawsuit filed May 7, 2003 in Brussels, Belgium charging him with "ordering war crimes and for not preventing others from committing them or for providing protection to the perpetrators." That, according to the 18 Iraqis and 2 Jordanians, who introduced a class action suit against Franks. The plaintiffs acknowledged that Franks acted on orders from higher authorities in the Bush II Administration, suggesting that others throughout the US military and US government should be included in the class action suit.

The 20 victims cite serious injuries or loss of relatives due to the "use of cluster bombs, attacks on civilians, including journalists, acts of aggression against health services and other Iraqi infrastructure, and looting protected by or under orders from the US Army". They also cite fear of the long-term effects of depleted uranium used by the US military forces in Iraq.

Belgian law gives that government the option of filing a case before the International Criminal Court (ICC) or forwarding it to the United States (country of origin of the accused). Since the United States did not ratify the ICC, it is not possible for the ICC to try Franks there for war crimes, and there is little chance he will face them here.

Franks wholeheartedly supported the war. He said that within hours of the 9/11 attacks, orders came down to him to prepare for war on the Taliban in Afghanistan and find Osama bin-Laden.

In his 30-year military career, Franks amassed a military record that shows a chest full of medals and ribbons, but he earned perhaps his most startling distinction after he retired. He made the first public statement of a Bush II Administration official in that martial law would replace the US Constitution after the next "terror" attack here in America. He just did not say how soon.

In the December 2003 issue of *Cigar Aficianado*, he stated that if the United States — or one of its allies — is hit with a weapon of mass destruction that inflicts large casualties, the US Constitution would be abandoned and a military state would result.

Regardless of the nature of such an attack — biological, chemical or nuclear weapons — Frank explained what would happen afterwards. *It means the potential of a weapon of mass destruction and a terrorist, massive, casualty-producing event somewhere in the Western world — it may be in the United States of America — that causes our population to question our own Constitution and to begin to militarize our country in order to avoid a repeat of another mass, casualty-producing event. This, in fact, then begins to unravel the fabric of our Constitution. Two steps, very, very important.*

Franks seems star-struck where Bush II is concerned, believing that his legacy will show him as a president of "high character and intelligence". He even uses the word "hero" in the same sentence with Bush. That, from a decorated general about a man who went AWOL in the National Guard, never participated in a military conflict, and who finds it easy to send American's youngest and brightest to die in an illegal war.

GENERAL RICHARD B. MYERS

Currently serving as the Chairman of the Joint Chiefs of Staff under Bush II, General Myers is the first line of military advice for Bush II, Rumsfeld and Rice. He was Acting Chairman during the attacks of 9/11. During the attacks, his unruffled demeanor was incongruous for the second highest military leader facing America's greatest terrorist tragedy. He claims to have been uninformed until the third plane hit the Pentagon.

The Pentagon had been overseeing the hijacked planes from the moment of the strike at the first WTC tower, yet not until the third strike was a decision made to send up fighter planes. By law, the fighters should have been up at 8:15AM. If they had, they might have diverted or shot down all of the hijacked planes.

Who and what kept the Air Force from following its normal procedures instead of waiting 1 hour and 20 minutes until after the damage was done? Why was Myers — in his position as the nation's Number Two military leader — left in the dark? Or was he?

The overriding question seems to be why did Myers tell NORAD to stand down on September 11, 2001 and not intercept airplanes headed for the World Trade Center? As Al Martin, retired Navy Lt. Commander and a political and military analyst, has pointed out, that question remains unanswered, as does the question about why Myers did not appear before the 9/11 Commission.

It is not that precedent had not been set for NORAD to intercept, even shoot down, civilian planes that ran astray of their normal routes. In 1998, a memo stated that, according to the FBI's intelligence gathering, a real threat existed in which terrorists would hijack airplanes and crash them into office buildings. That memo eventually landed on John Ashcroft's desk.

Then-President Clinton instituted extensive upgrades in protocols governing national security, NORAD's status in major US cities, and NORAD's ability to intercept and shoot down civilian planes off course, without the permission of higher authorities.

With all those protocols in place, the Bush II and his phalanx of neocons ignored them on September 11, 2001. Myers became Joint Chiefs of Staff on October 1, 2001.

In the more recent fiasco in Iraq, Myers once referred to Fallujah as a "rat's nest." Considering what most people do when they find rats, one wonders what kind of commands he issued for dealing with those in Fallujah.

Major General Antonio Taguba led an inquiry into Abu Ghraib Prison that found "numerous incidents of sadistic, blatant and wanton criminal abuses" inflicted on Iraqi prisoners. His assessment showed how flaws in the command structure created a vacuum of authority that allowed violations to take place. At the time, 10 Iraqi prisons, including Abu Ghraib, held over 8,000 prisoners.

Although the Pentagon refuses to provide a total run-down on the number of prisoners, unofficial estimates indicate that the US currently detain 300 prisoners in Afghanistan and another 600 or more in Guantanamo.

The Geneva Convention set forth in October 1950 rules for the protection of victims of war, as follows:

> *For all persons taking no active part in hostilities shall in all circumstances be treated humanely, without regard to race, color, religion, sex, birth or wealth. Prohibited are: (1) violence to life and person (including murder, mutilation, cruel treatment and torture, (2) taking of hostages, (3) outrages upon personal dignity (humiliating and degrading treatment), and (4) passing sentences and carrying out executions without previous judgment by a court.* Further note indicates that the wounded and sick are to be cared for.

In light of all that surfaced in recent weeks, the US military has violated all of the Geneva Conventions. The military is a stickler for using the proper chain of command in reporting problems. Each level reports up to the next level. The buck stops at the top, Donald Rumsfeld, but accountability falls on all levels of command, including the nation's highest-ranking officer, General Myers.

LT. GENERAL RICARDO SANCHEZ

General Ricardo Sanchez served as the Iraq Commander during the time when rampant prisoner abuses took place in prisons all over Iraq. Consequently, he — and others under his command — symbolize the vacuum of authority in which unsupervised officers took power trips and exacted abuse and humiliation on countless innocent people.

The Pentagon refuses to add Sanchez to the culpability list for the abuse of prisoners and detainees. Suspicion remains for Sanchez, however, as well as for Brigadier General Janis Karpinski, who directed operations at Abu Ghraib Prison, where the majority of abuses occurred. Major General Antonio Taguba laid much of the blame on Karpinski's performance. He recommended that she be relieved of command and formally reprimanded. Instead, Sanchez sent her back to the United States with a "memorandum of admonishment" on January 17, 2004.

In Taguba's report that documented abuse, he found no evidence that Karpinski ensured that the military officers under her command knew about the Geneva Conventions, which protect both prisoners of war and civilian detainees during armed conflict.

Sanchez's policy for detainees and prisoners called for the use of guard dogs, shackling, nudity and other aggressive techniques. When General Miller, commander of the US detention center in Guantanamo Bay, Cuba, went to Iraq to reinforce intelligence gathering at Abu Ghraib, he recommended using guard dogs to frighten detainees. Sanchez, the top military officer in Iraq, approved the guard dog policy.

On June 30, 2004, Sanchez faced a scheduled change in rotation of duty, leaving Iraq to another general. Bush II, Rumsfeld and Powell offered praise and admiration for Sanchez's performance in Iraq. What else would they do? Admit Sanchez was part of the wrongdoing and cover-up?

MAJOR GENERAL GEOFFREY MILLER

General Miller presided over interrogation of prisoners at Guantanamo Bay's Camp X-Ray until recently, when he accepted reassignment to Iraq. Reports continue to surface that interrogation protocol at Guantanamo included abuse, humiliation and torture, similar to what the public has seen in Iraq. Videotapes of interrogations there recently came to the attention of Congress, which demanded that Guantanamo turn the tapes over to lawmakers for review.

Miller clearly called for the use of military police in interrogations, thereby helping to create the environment that resulted in subsequent abuse and torture. The Department of Defense authorized the interrogation techniques for Guantanamo, including forcing prisoners and detainees to strip naked, listen to loud music, endure bright lights and suffer sleep deprivation.

It is no secret that the United States Army has taught torture and assassination methods to military officers around the world, especially those from Latin America at the School of the Americas (SOA), aka School of the Assassins. According to *The Washington Post*, US Army intelligence manuals used to train military officers advocated executions, torture, blackmail and other forms of coercion against insurgents.

Graduates of SOA include some of Latin America's most notorious human rights violators, including those who participated in Salvadoran death squads, assassinated six Jesuit priests, and killed students and other innocent civilians. From 1982-91, SOA trained more than 60,000 officers in these tactics.

It does not take a rocket scientist to figure that what we teach others, we also perform on prisoners and detainees under our control. Americans, for the most part, do not realize that they fund a school that instructs others in mental and physical torture, humiliation, and murder. Individuals like Fr. Roy Bourjois of the SOA Watch have long lobbied for closing the SOA.

In the fall of 2003, Cambone sent Miller to Iraq to aid in making changes to effect more successful interrogations. "We had, then, in Iraq, a large body of people who had been captured on the battlefield that we had to gain intelligence for force protection purposes," said Cambone at the time. "And he [Miller] was asked to go over there, at my encouragement, to take a look at the situation as it existed there. And he made his recommendations."

Cambone decided to use Miller after he saw the report on Camp X-Ray that indicated three-fourths of the 600 Taliban and al-Qaeda suspects were becoming "compliant" and offering intelligence tips.

After Miller's visit to Iraq, prisoner abuse rose dramatically until news about it broke worldwide in the spring of 2004. Miller, newly appointed commander of Abu Ghraib Prison — and other prisons — in Iraq, is in charge of cleaning up the mess to which he most likely contributed.

LT. GENERAL WILLIAM "JERRY" BOYKIN

General Boykin makes no bones about it. He truly believes that the God of his extreme Christian fundamentalism outweighs and outshines the God of Islam. The fact that he serves as Rumsfeld's appointee to secure the prisoner interrogation process in a country where many of the prisoners and detainees are Muslim seems inappropriate, at least.

Boykin is Deputy Undersecretary of Defense Intelligence under Cambone (remember, the "henchman") and one tied closely to Rumsfeld through a long-standing friendship. He believes that the War on Terrorism is a religious war between Judeo-Christians and Satan (Islam, to Boykin). He also believes that Bush II became President because that was what God wanted and that his orders come not from his father, Bush I, but from his other Father, God. If you believe that, we have some property in…oh, you know.

In a speech to a religious group in Oregon, he explained why he thinks Muslims hate the United States. It is "because we are a Christian nation, because our foundation and roots are Judeo-Christian. . .and the enemy is a guy named Satan. Our own spiritual enemy will only be defeated if we come against them in the name of Jesus." With ignorant statements like that, Boykin lowers the bar considerably.

That statement brings to mind the story of one US military interrogator in Iraq who forced a Muslim prisoner to denounce Islam and thank Jesus that he was alive. Now we know who prompts officers to use such tactics. It is no wonder that Arab Americans and Muslim Americans have long protested Boykin.

A 30-year veteran in the US Army's Delta Force, the CIA and Army Special Forces, Boykin is just one of a host of right-wing Christian Rapture fanatics occupying the White House. Whatever happened to separation of church and state? Evidently Bush, Boykin and his other Christian fundamentalist cronies never read the statement of John Adams, second President of the United States, "…the government of the United States or America is not in any sense founded on the Christian Religion…"

L. PAUL BREMER

Americans cannot teach democracy to the world until they restore their own.
William Greider, journalist

Paul Bremer, Administrator of the Iraq Coalition Provisional Authority (CPA) until June 30, 2004, seemed to reflect the old adage, "If you are not working on the solution, you must be part of the problem." More and more Iraqis feel that Bremer has been part of the problem.

Some of the statements he made in late 2003 now ring hollow. Consider his statement of September 2, 2003: "The Iraqi people are now free. And they do not have to worry about the secret police coming after them in the middle of the night, and they don't have to worry about their husbands and brothers being taken off and shot or their wives being taken to rape rooms. Those days are over." By then, abuse scandals were brewing throughout Iraq.

Then, on November 26, 2003, he declared that the situation in Iraq was "getting better." One wonders where he was standing to see any improvement, even as the prisoner abuse was building.

Perhaps his naivete about judging when improvements were gaining a foothold comes from his ignorance of Iraq's land and its people. A former senior State Department official, who worked with Bremer, once noted, "What he knows about Iraq could not quite fill a thimble."

In direct contrast to Bremer's brilliant introduction of *Baghdad Now*, a psy-ops paper filled with fluff about freedom of the press and such, Bremer called for the shutdown of Muqtada al-Sadr's newspaper. Although al-Sadr was a militant Shiite who condemned Americans for attacks on Iraqi civilians, he resisted the occupation through nonviolent means. So much for freedom of the press.

Bremer's shutdown fueled the resistance. It was not his first mistake as America's official envoy to Iraq. When he first arrived there, he fired 40,000 Iraqi soldiers, refusing to give them their pensions in the process. At least, he let them keep their guns.

Part of Bremer's problem is common to most members of the Bush Administration. They are ignorant of the Arab culture and clueless about the people of Iraq. Some blame the majority of Iraq's current problems on Bremer, accusing him of destroying the country. Even in his attempt to rebuild the infrastructure, he threw the country into chaos.

The laundry list of grievances grows longer with each passing day. Even before news of the prisoner abuse scandals circled the globe, corruption and crises were order of the day in Iraq. Corruption underscored reconstruction contracts (Halliburton and Bechtel landed huge government contracts without facing a bidding war). Security was lax and looting persisted throughout the land. Iraq's borders remained unsecured, allowing unwanted terrorists and unregulated imports to gain entry.

With all Bush's talk about bestowing democracy on the Iraqi people, Bremer excluded Iraqi companies, still hurting from US-imposed sanctions, from competing for reconstruction work. People in Iraq are hurting from the war, from the effects of sanctions and from widespread unemployment. Most people cannot make a living wage.

Rebuilding a war-torn nation requires touching hearts and changing lives. Bremer has ignored that need in his charge to rebuild Iraq. The result has been even more devastating than the war itself. Factions, formerly in enemy camps, have merged to fight the American occupiers. Many Iraqi civilians, who are honest, hard-working people, feel betrayed by Bremer and the United States.

Under Bremer's watch, the worst US military scandal surfaced. Bush Administration neocons and military bigwigs ran for cover or passed the blame. Nevertheless, the International Committee of the Red Cross delivered its 24-page report about US military/intelligence abuse of Iraqi prisoners to

Paul Bremer and Lt. General Ricardo Sanchez in February 2004, well before the news broke worldwide.

Although Bremer's term in Iraq ends on June 30, 2004, he has his plate full between now and then. In March, he passed a law that opened Iraq's economy to foreign ownership. Under the terms of the interim constitution, Iraq's next government cannot change that law.

Bremer also established several independent regulators, drastically eroding the power of Iraqi ministries. Regulators would prevent people such as communications minister from canceling licenses that Bremer awarded to foreign companies to operate the Iraq national broadcast system.

The Coalition Provisional Authority also confirmed that after June 30, the US Embassy would administer the $18.4 billion the United States has earmarked for reconstruction over the next five years. This decision leaves the Iraqi government with little say about the complete redesign and reconstruction of their own infrastructure. The funds, according to Retired Rear Admiral David Nash, are "a gift from the American people to the people of Iraq." He directs the agency that administers the funds.

Yet another of Bremer's tricks to protect US interests in Iraq was the start of construction by US engineers on 14 military bases for 110,000 soldiers, who will remain in Iraq for two or more years. [Some say we will never leave Iraq. You do not build 14 military bases for a one- or two-year stay.] The Iraqi government did not invite continued US military presence, but that does not seem to matter. The bases, according to Brig. General Mark Kimmitt, US deputy chief of operations in Iraq, serve as "a blueprint for how we could operate in the Middle East."

Bremer also ordered that even after the United States turned control over to the Iraqi interim government, the Iraqi armed forces would answer to the US Commander in charge. UN Security Council Resolution 1511 puts US forces in charge of Iraq's security until "the completion of the political process" there. A legal reading of that clause could interpret that since the political process in Iraq is ongoing, so should the US military presence in Iraq.

Bremer's bag of tricks grew larger. He announced that the CPA would further constrain the Iraqi military by appointing a national security advisor, similar to Condoleeza Rice in authority, who will remain in office for five years. That term extends far beyond the timetable for Iraq to have made its transition to a democracy.

Bremer kindly left the Iraqis to handle their own hospitals, however, in their pitiful conditions and with chronic drug shortages. US Health and Human Services Secretary Tommy Thompson revealed the low priority status of Iraq's hospitals when he stated that Iraq could fix its hospitals if the Iraqis "just washed their hands and cleaned the crap off the walls."

Unless the most recent scandals radically change the US presence in Iraq, the land that we invaded with the gift of democracy will not be free for a very long time, if ever. The US presence there will be enormous. The military will have its 14 bases, and the US Embassy will be the largest in the world. The US will have authority over the Iraqi military, as well as its security, economic policy, and reconstruction of its infrastructure. Not to mention control of the oil, which is the reason we went there in the first place.

Why do more and more Iraqis hate the United States presence in their country? It seems that the war did the least damage. The occupation has brought the most serious toll — shattered hopes of the Iraqis themselves.

The ballyhooed US turnover of authority to the Iraqi government may or may not succeed. Many Iraqis will not accept any government official that maintains close ties to the United States government, one they have grown to distrust and resent. The CIA puppet head of Iraq's new government will ensure the US presence there.

JOHN NEGROPONTE

Clearly one of Washington's most controversial figures, John Negroponte is the newly appointed Ambassador to Iraq following Paul Bremer's stint in that capacity. His post immediately before this appointment was Bush II's Ambassador to the United Nations. His first ambassador post, however, brought him notoriety that still haunts him and raised questions on Capitol Hill about the appropriateness of his newest appointment. That was when he served as Ambassador to Honduras from 1981-85.

Along with Elliott Abrams and Otto Reich, Negroponte was complicit in a bloody scandal, the work of condoned death squads that tortured and killed civilians at random in El Salvador

During his ambassadorship in Honduras, so many US military bases and weapons cropped up there that the country earned the nickname the USS Honduras. Poverty raged, yet US military spending skyrocketed from $3.9 million in 1980 to $77.4 million in 1984.

The Honduran Army, especially its notorious Battalion 316, engaged in widespread abuses of human rights. Kidnappings, torture and assassinations were the order of the day. According to Honduras Ambassador Jack Binns, his predecessor, Negroponte worked closely with the violators and covered up their crimes.

The horror stories of torture and execution became commonplace in both Central and South America in the 1980s. Consider the statement of the Head of the US Office of Public Safety (OPS) regarding class instructions in the art of torture in Uruguay: *I can teach you about torture, but sooner or later, you'll have to get involved yourself. You'll have to lay on your hands and try it yourself. The precise pain…in the precise place…in the precise amount for the desired effect.*

In Baghdad, Negroponte will be the principle adviser to the Iraqi government, in control of the billions in American aid going to Iraq and, as the US Ambassador to Iraq, he will oversee the 3,000-person Embassy there, the largest in the world. Thanks to the US taxpayers, of course.

KENNETH ADELMAN

A White House spokesman and member of the Defense Policy Board in the Pentagon, Kenneth Adelman's right-wing activities date back to the 1970s when he served on the Committee on the Present Danger. His mentor is Donald Rumsfeld, whom he served as Assistant from 1975 to 1977. He served as Deputy Permanent Representative to the UN in the Reagan Administration from 1981-83.

More recently, he joined others in signing an April 3, 2002 letter to Bush II calling for regime change in Iraq and increased support for Israel. In one of his gaps in clear thinking, Adelman predicted that liberating Iraq would be a "cakewalk", boasting that Bush did not need to "amass rinky-dink nations as 'coalition partners' to convince the Washington establishment that we're right."

He also went out on a limb about Saddam Hussein's supposed weapons of mass destruction, even predicting that they most likely would be found near Tikrit and Baghdad, "because they're the most protected places with the best troops. I have no doubt we're going to find big stores of weapons of mass destruction." Wonder what he thinks now.

A signatory for PNAC and guest commentator on Murdoch's FOX News, Adelman added right wing clout to the pro-war lobby. In an article written in 2002, "The Ankle Biters", he chided Arab nations for criticizing US Middle East policy and referred to the Arab World as a declining civilization.

Before criticizing us, Arabs should read the UN's 'Arab Human Development Report', and realize they have no grounds to criticize successful societies. With a collective population roughly that of the United States, the 22 Arab states have a total GDP less than Spain's, with exports (without oil) less than Norway's, and per capita income less than one-sixth that of Western democracies, no visible presence in the main arenas of human excellence today — Nobel Prize winners, World Cup finalists, Olympic medal winners, breakthrough scientists, leading historians, international business tycoons — no civil or political rights of a democracy or decent society. These are the hallmarks of a declining civilization.

JOHN POINDEXTER

Another Bush II appointee with a criminal past, John Poindexter became Director of the Pentagon's newly created Information Awareness Office (IAO), which secretly gathers and centralizes intelligence from the Internet, as well as from telephone and fax lines, about as many Americans as possible. The ultimate goal is to combine all private databases about US citizens into a central government database. Information such as credit card purchases, travel, medical history, and employment would be included. [QUICK QUIZ: Name another country in history where similar activities took place. HINT: Europe.]

More than just creating a repository of information about American citizens, the IAO supplies federal officials with "instant" analysis on emails and telephone conversations throughout the entire country. That is spying right here at home.

The IAO is one of two branches of DARPA, the Pentagon's Defense Advanced Research Projects Agency. To understand the connection to its current mission, another agency, ARPA, previously created the Internet.

A retired US Navy admiral, who lost his job as Reagan's National Security Advisor, Poindexter was convicted on multiple felony counts — conspiracy, lying to Congress, defrauding the government, and destroying evidence in the Iran-Contra scandal. He sold weapons illegally to Iran, then funneled the money illegally to Nicaragua's Contra Army. His conviction was overturned a year later, because he had been granted immunity from prosecution for his testimony before Congress.

Poindexter amassed impressive credentials before he strayed in the Reagan Administration. He graduated at the top of his class at the Naval Academy, received a Ph.D. in physics, became America's best-educated naval officer, commanded missile destroyers, and won plenty of medals in the process. From there, he acquired a long list of high-tech positions that advanced his knowledge of clandestine intelligence gathering.

After the attempt on President Reagan's life in 1981, Poindexter reviewed White House security and so impressed Reagan that he made Poindexter his National Security Advisor. He participated in the development of FEMA Executive Orders for issuance during Martial Law, should another terrorist attack occur in America.

He and Oliver North got involved in the Iran-Contra scandal, which hit its peak in 1986, when authorities charged him with several felonies. Ironically, the authorities caught him and his cohorts when, after carefully deleting 5,000 incriminating emails, they forgot to destroy the backup tapes.

The Iran-Contra scandal was not Poindexter's first brush with illegal activities. Although he never faced charges for it, he participated in cocaine trafficking to raise money for the contras. He brazenly admitted, "I made a very deliberate decision not to tell the President so that I could insulate him from the decision and provide some future deniability for the President if it ever leaked out."

There you have it. An ex-felon in charge of snooping on American citizens. All protected nice and legal under the umbrella of the War on Terrorism.

JAMES SCHLESINGER, JR.

Yet another pro-Israel extremist, James Schlesinger, Jr. is a member of the Defense Policy Board and a Pentagon advisor. He joined the chorus of those who consistently advocated bombing Iraq.

As Secretary of Defense under both Nixon and Ford, he earned a reputation for being tough and blunt and amassed considerable knowledge about matters of national security. He advocated maintaining a strong defense establishment as a means of deterrence and on building a healthy Department of Defense budget. He was especially keen on making certain the US military power balanced that of any opponent in the world.

In 1973, the Yom Kippur War between Israel, Egypt, and Syria gave Schlesinger an opportunity to help Israel. He explained that initially the United States decided to avoid involvement, thinking Israel would quickly win the war. When it became apparent that might not happen, due to Israel's inability to re-supply its forces, the United States stepped in.

Schlesinger fielded criticism that the US delayed getting involved to save face with the Arab states. Eventually a cease-fire ended the conflict, but because of the US effort to aid Israel, the Arab members of OPEC cut off oil shipments to the US for several months.

It might be appropriate here to add a quote from former President Dwight Eisenhower (and former 5-Star General and Allied Supreme Commander in World War II), taken from his farewell address to the nation on January 17, 1961:

> *In the councils of government, we must guard against the acquisition of unwarranted influence, whether sought or unsought, by the military-industrial complex. The potential for the disastrous rise of misplaced power exists and will persist. We must never let the weight of this combination endanger our liberties or democratic processes. We should take nothing for granted. The prospect of domination of the nation's scholars by Federal*

employment, project allocations and the power of money is ever present — and is gravely to be regarded.

During Schlesinger's term in the Ford Administration, he locked horns with then-Secretary of State Henry Kissinger and that problem, along with others, including his insistence on increased defense spending, led to his dismissal by Ford in November 1975.

FRANK CARLUCCI

Chairman and CEO of the Washington-based Carlyle Group, Frank Carlucci's past government posts and his close friendship with Rumsfeld has helped him expand Carlyle's defense industry portfolio. In short, the Group is making a fortune on the War on Terrorism as an insider of the "iron triangle" — defense, government and industry.

The Carlyle Group is one of the world's most powerful and secretive companies. A private investment company, Carlyle has had strong ties to Saudi Arabia. Carlucci, along with Armitage and Abrams and others, comprised the special interagency group known as RAG-1, created to manage and control the liability of the Iran-Contra operation. In more apparently honorable posts, Carlucci served as Secretary of Defense under Reagan and Deputy CIA Director under Carter.

Prior to September 11, 2001, Osama bin Laden's family members belonged to the Carlyle Group and, like the other members, stood to reap a bundle fighting, ironically, someone in their own family. Joint participation in that group strengthened the ties between the bin Ladens and the Bushes.

On 9/11, Carlyle's annual investor meeting took place at the Ritz Carlton in Washington. Present were Bush I, then a Carlyle senior advisor, members of the bin Laden family and others. The tumbling towers of the World Trade Center ended the bin Laden's possibility of reaping a windfall, as public criticism compelled them to dissolve their assets in Carlyle. Moneymaking makes strange bedfellows, indeed.

One example shows how strong the ties were between Carlyle and the bin Ladens. On 9/11, although all commercial flights had been grounded, the US made one exception — the flights, arranged by Prince Bandar with the blessing of the White House, to evacuate members of the bin Laden family. It is interesting to note that unlike Israelis, who received advance notice about the World Trade Center attack, giving the time to depart, the bin Laden family apparently did not know.

Members of the Carlyle Group, officially worth over $13 billion, include former world leaders and Washington insiders, and all of them stand to make billions in the War on Terrorism, including the wars in Afghanistan and Iraq. In addition to Frank Carlucci, members have included George Bush I, James Baker III (former Secretary of State and Secretary of the Treasury), and former Prime Minister of England, John Major.

HALLIBURTON

David Lesar is the Chairman, President and CEO of Halliburton, the Texas energy giant, for which Richard Cheney served as its CEO before becoming Bush II's Vice President. In 2003, Cheney received more than $175,000 in deferred pay from Halliburton.

In a recent turn of events, insider news reveals that Cheney, despite public refutations, greased the mechanism for Halliburton to win billions of dollars in no-bid contracts, making his former employer the largest beneficiary of Oil War II. Those billions, known as "war profiteering", continue to grow as the quagmire continues in Iraq.

In its June 7, 2004 issue, *TIME* magazine uncovered evidence of Cheney's lingering involvement with Halliburton. The article notes than in September 2003 on NBC's "Meet the Press", Cheney refuted any involvement in hefty government contracts secured by Halliburton. "Of course not...And as Vice President, I have absolutely no influence of, involvement of, knowledge of in any way, shape or form of contracts led by the [Army] Corps of Engineers or anybody else in the Federal Government." Right.

The Cheney-Halliburton relationship did not end when he left that company's helm to help secure the presidency for George W. Bush. Halliburton has not only profited by the Iraq War; it has also heavily influenced the energy policy of the Bush Administration. If not, why would Cheney refuse to reveal the participants and contents of the energy meetings he held after becoming Vice President?

The other problem that still plagues Cheney is his financial ties to Halliburton. After receiving a multi-million dollar bonus for his work as CEO, despite its less than outstanding quality, Cheney continues to receive "deferred pay" for his services to Halliburton through a special arrangement. It is inappropriate, at least, for the Vice President to continue receiving money from a former employer that receives billions of dollars in contracts from the Pentagon.

Halliburton's multi-billion-dollar contract RIO (Restore Iraqi Oil) is just one of its benefits of the Iraq War. Since the war ended, Halliburton and its subsidiary Kellogg Brown Root have been awarded almost $6 billion in contracts for work in Iraq, and have some 24,000 employees working in the Gulf region. Halliburton charged hundreds of millions of dollars for meals for US troops in Iraq that were never delivered.

BECHTEL

Chairman and CEO of the Bechtel Group, Riley Bechtel's close connections to Dick Cheney surely contributed to the company's enormously lucrative contracts to help rebuild Iraqi infrastructure. The company's contracts run through 2005.

For years, Bechtel has enjoyed a close relationship with Republican foreign policymakers, globally and in Iraq. Many of today's war hawks spent a couple of years in the 1980s trying to get Saddam to sign an oil pipeline contract. Even though Saddam was gassing Iranians at the same time, people like Donald Rumsfeld had some quality face-time with Saddam pitching a plan that would benefit, more than anyone else, Bechtel and possibly Saddam.

Rumsfeld flew to Baghdad twice as Reagan's special envoy. Much of the business had nothing more to do than advance Bechtel's business. Then-Secretary of State George Schultz, who joined the Reagan Administration straight out of the CEO chair at Bechtel, devised the plan for Rumsfeld to pitch on behalf of building an oil pipeline from Iraq to Jordan in December 1983.

Saddam liked the idea, but he was concerned about the possibility of an Israeli attack. Rumsfeld wrote to Schultz, "I said I could understand that there would need to be some sort of arrangements that would give those involved confidence that it would not be easily vulnerable. (This may be an issue to raise with Israel at the appropriate time.)"

For the next two years, Reagan officials, Bechtel and pipeline promoters tried to soothe Saddam's concerns about Israel. At the same time, the US government condemned the use of chemical weapons used in the Iran-Iraq War. Rumsfeld met a second time in Baghdad to promote the Bechtel pipeline scheme. That meeting took place the same day that UN fact finders confirmed that Saddam gassed Iranian troops.

The whirlwind of activities surrounding Reagan, Rumsfeld, Bechtel and Hussein produced a number of shady deals. One agent promised Israeli Prime Minister Shimon Peres and his Labor Party secret access to the pipeline profits. Reagan officials considered other ideas, like committing defense and foreign aid as collateral in case Israel attacked the pipeline. Whatever it took to calm Hussein's fears, the Reagan Administration considered it.

None of it mattered in the end. Two years later, Hussein rejected Bechtel's proposal, because Turkey and Saudi Arabia offered him better deals. The Reagan and Bush I Administrations eventually secured contracts for Bechtel with Hussein to build an enormous chemical plant outside Baghdad.

In 2002, when Saddam Hussein submitted his list of corporate suppliers for chemical weapon development to the United Nations, Bechtel's name was on the list. Construction of the chemical plant ceased with Hussein's invasion of Kuwait.

Gulf War I ended the oil relations between the US and Iraq. Surely, it pained Rumsfeld, Bechtel and others to see Iraq make contracts with China, France and Russia.

The bottom line in this story is that when the United States government wants another country's oil, no matter how dictatorial its leader is, we will do business. If that leader chooses not to do business with the US, he becomes our mortal enemy, just as Saddam Hussein became.

Bechtel stands ready to accept yet another lucrative contract — building a new maximum-security prison in Baghdad after the United States razes Abu Ghraib Prison. Nothing like getting rid of reminders of US military scandal.

IRVING KRISTOL

Irving Kristol was part of the "New York Intellectuals", the group of critics mainly of Eastern European Jewish descent. Kristol, considered the 'godfather' of neoconservatism and Norman Podhoretz, its grandfather, are, in part, responsible for grooming the neocons, who now surround Bush II and who have created the mess we face in Iraq and around the world.

In the late 1930s, he studied at City College of New York. From 1947-1952, he served as managing editor of *Commentary* magazine, later known as the neocon bible.

By the late 1960s, he shifted politically from left to right, in part because of his concern that liberals gave into excesses and anti-Americanism.

Neoconservatism, according to James Zogby, president of the Arab American Institute, is the "secular political philosophy that defined the reaction of a group of liberals to what they felt was the Democratic Party's policy of appeasement toward the Soviet Union — most especially the USSR's treatment of its Jewish population and its relations with the Arab World."

Influenced by Leo Strauss, a professor of philosophy at the University of Chicago, Kristol built the intellectual framework of neoconservatism. Strauss assumed the Machiavellian proposition that force and fraud are necessary tools to achieve prosperity. He believed that only a militantly patriotic state could ward off aggression, and that some external threat — found or manufactured — could create that patriotism.

Kristol founded and edited such journals as *The Public Interest* and *The National Interest*. He is a fellow at the American Enterprise Institute and author of many books, including *Neoconservatism: The Autobiography of an Idea*.

Irving Kristol founded PNAC in 1997, uniting into a powerful alliance Dick Cheney and Donald Rumsfeld, Christian Right leaders and neocons. He counts Richard Perle among his most loyal followers.

He is the father of William Kristol, editor of Rupert Murdoch's *The Weekly Standard* and frequently quoted neocon. William authored a letter sent to Bush II on April 3, 2002. The letter, signed by 31 neocons, states that the "United States and Israel share a common enemy", urges Bush to no longer pressure Israel to negotiate with the Palestinians, and beseeches him to lend "full support to Israel." It also urges Bush to "accelerate plans for removing Saddam Hussein from power in Iraq." The signers of the letter concluded by saying, "Israel's fight against terrorism is our fight. Israel's victory is an important part of our victory."

NORMAN PODHORETZ

A founding father of the neocons, Norman Podhoretz studies, writes and speaks about social, cultural and international issues. From 1960-1995, he served as Editor-in-Chief of *Commentary* magazine, a neocon journal published by the American Jewish Committee. At *Commentary*, he gave such neocon rising stars as Daniel Pipes and Jeane Kirkpatrick a place to expound on their ideology of global supremacy.

Podhoretz was part of the Coalition for Democratic Majority, founded in 1973 by US Senator Henry "Scoop" Jackson and other intervention-minded Democrats. He is a member of PNAC and the Council on Foreign Relations. He is a Fellow at the Hudson Institute, financed by the Bradley, Olin and Scaife Foundations.

He and his wife, Midge Decter, as leaders of the Committee on the Present Danger in 1980, worked with Rumsfeld to kill détente and promote the political rise of Ronald Reagan. Their son, John, is a columnist for Murdoch-owned *New York Post* and appears as a frequent guest on Murdoch-owned FOX News.

Podhoretz is the author of nine books. *Breaking Ranks*, published in 1979, argues that Israel's survival is crucial to US military strategy. He signed the April 3, 2002 letter to President Bush II, along with 30 others, calling for regime change in Iraq and increased support of Israel.

R. JAMES WOOLSEY

It isn't only Gestapo maniacs who do inhuman things to people. We [the CIA] are responsible for doing inhuman things to a massive scale of people all over the world. – John Stockwell, former CIA official

The CIA Director under President Clinton, James Woolsey founded Americans for Victory over Terrorism with religious right spokesman William

Bennett and Paul Bremer. After 9/11, Woolsey sounded the alarm that Saddam Hussein was behind those terrorist attacks, as well as the anthrax scare that followed, and he was the greatest threat to America.

His words carried a lot of weight in sending US troops off to overthrow Saddam Hussein's regime. He used Murdoch-owned talk shows to further the war hawks' position publicly. The White House all too eagerly heeded his call.

Woolsey maintains that World War IV, the War on Terrorism, is against three enemies: the religious rules of Iran, the "fascists" of Iraq and Syria, and Islamic extremists.

A controversial high-profile hawk, Woolsey is a prominent member of the Defense Policy Board of the Pentagon and an influential advisor to Bush II. He is also director of the Washington-based Paladin Capital, a private equity company, set up only three months after 9/11 as a business opportunity that 'offers substantial promise for homeland security investment.' It also stands to make millions from the War on Terror.

Woolsey, who has Israeli connections, co-signed the April 3, 2002 letter to President Bush II. In one part of the letter, it states, "In the war on terrorism, we cannot condemn some terrorists while claiming that other terrorists are potential partners for peace."

That position overlooks the fact that we have propped up dictators the world over in the guise of peace and democracy, only to have those dictators murder countless civilians before losing their grip on power. In more than 30 countries in which we have attempted to bring democratic order, not one has resulted in a democracy.

Among many in the Bush II Administration who fell for the weapons of mass destruction notion, Woolsey voiced opposition to containing Saddam Hussein. *Saddam wants to dominate that portion of the world, its oil supplies and his neighbors, and he is working hard on weapons of mass destruction and ballistic missiles in order to do it.*

DANIEL PIPES

A Likudnik Jewish intellectual and academic, Daniel Pipes reflects some of the most extremist views about US policy in the Middle East. In short, he believes that the only way peace will reign in that region is through a decisive military victory for Israel. He shuns the ideas of negotiation, compromise and diplomacy. "What war had achieved for Israel, diplomacy has undone," he told a Zionist conference in Washington, DC.

Pipes believes that the Israeli military must force a "change of heart" by the Palestinians in the West Bank and Gaza. Sap their will to fight, leaving them no choice but complete surrender. "How can a change of heart be achieved? It is achieved by an Israeli victory and a Palestinian defeat. The Palestinians need to be defeated even more than Israel needs to defeat them."

His views of an Israeli-Palestinian solution were more extremist than those of Bush II or Sharon, who accepted a "road map" for peace. They do not represent the views of the majority of Israelis, either. An April 2003 poll by Tel Aviv University revealed that 65 percent support the road map, including 58 percent of Sharon's Likud Party.

Early in 2003, Bush II's nomination of Pipes to the board of the United States Institute of Peace, a Congressionally sponsored think tank dedicated to the "peaceful resolution of international conflicts" left many people scratching their heads. Pipes and peace is an oxymoron.

Consider his views on Islam. "Most Muslims, unfortunately, are suspect," he noted in a recent book, "although only 10 to 15 percent are militant. If Muslims have jobs in the military, law enforcement or diplomacy, they need to be watched for connections to terrorism." He finds problems with Muslim immigration. "All immigrants bring exotic customs and attitudes, but Muslim customs are more troublesome than most."

Pipes traces his personal views on the Israeli-Palestinian conflict to the early days of the struggle. In 1923, Ze'ev Jabotinsky, one of the fathers of Israeli right-wing ideology, wrote that no peace would be achieved until the Arabs in Israel were psychologically crushed. "As long as the Arabs preserve a gleam of hope that they will succeed in getting rid of us, nothing in the world can cause them to relinquish that hope."

Then, in 1936, David Ben-Gurion, who later became Israel's first Prime Minister, affirmed Jabotinsky's sentiments. *For only after total despair on the part of the Arabs, a despair that will come not only from the failure of the disturbances and the attempt at rebellion, but also as a consequence of our growth as a country, may the Arabs possibly acquiesce in a Jewish state in Israel.*

In 1990, Pipes dismissed the failed Oslo peace process and the underlying reasons for the road map. He said it was either "naive or duplicitous" to think that two states could exist between the Mediterranean Sea and the Jordan River. He has revised that hard-line attitude, admitting that a two-state solution could work but only after Palestinians surrender.

Pipes was one of 31 individuals who wrote President Bush II on April 3, 2002, pleading with him to oust Saddam Hussein from power in Iraq and increase support of Israel. How many more billions do they want out of the American taxpayers?

Three groups in particular embrace those extremist views today — right wing political parties in Israel, American Jewish supporters of the Israeli settlement movement, and evangelical Christians. The Interfaith Zionist

Leadership Summit, held in May 2003 in Washington, DC brought these groups together, and gave Pipes a standing ovation after his rousing speech.

Pipes recently helped push HR 3077 through Congress, with equal determination to see its way through the US Senate. That bill would establish a committee to make sure that college and university instructors teach nothing that is against Israel. Like others currently under consideration, this bill undermines the American right of free speech.

JOHN R. BOLTON

In 2001, the Bush II neocons gave Secretary of State Colin Powell someone he could just as soon do without — John R. Bolton. His brash ways and harsh attitudes fall outside Powell's more diplomatic views, not to mention those of mainstream America.

A neocon hawk, Bolton must never have taken a course in winning friends and influencing people. He is one of the leaders in undermining trust in the US government by countries around the world.

As Undersecretary of State for Arms Control and International Security Affairs, Bolton directs and coordinates arms control policy, foreign assistance programs, and military assistance programs for the State Department. Based on his background and belief system, Bolton stands to do more harm than good.

He served as Vice President at the American Enterprise Institute, in the Justice Department under Reagan and in Bush I's State Department. Along the way, he opposed many programs that he now oversees, such as the Anti-Ballistic Missile Treaty, the Comprehensive Nuclear Test Ban treaty and the International Criminal Court (ICC). His efforts to destroy the effectiveness of the ICC furthered European and third world resentment of the United States.

Sometimes, his campaigns backfire. Thanks to his undiplomatic tactics, a record number of countries signed and ratified the Rome Treaty, rapidly advancing the establishment of the ICC.

He has been unequivocal in his disdain for the United Nations. In 1994 he stated, "There is no such thing as the United Nations. If the UN Secretariat Building in New York lost 10 stories, it wouldn't make a bit of difference."

Bolton has made a career out of bashing and defying the United Nations, most recently in his staunch support of the Iraq War. He is a leading proponent of Bush II's Axis of Evil, broadening it to include Cuba and Libya.

Bolton, like his fellow neocons, makes war an obsession. Senator Jesse Helms endorsed Bolton's appointment. "John Bolton is the kind of man with whom I would want to stand at Armageddon, if it should be my lot to be on hand for what is forecast to be the final battle between good and evil."

RODERICK PAIGE

Secretary of Education in Bush II Cabinet, Roderick Paige's responsibility is to implement the "No Child Left Behind" (NCLB) educational reform program that Bush II touted when he ran as the "education candidate" in 2000. In reality, this program has left many children behind, contributed to the "dumbing down" of America's children, and left public schools impoverished and in shambles.

Recently Paige — the nation's top education official — referred to the 2.7 million-member National Education Association an organization of terrorists. Although he later apologized, he lit another fire in the process. He agreed that calling the NEA a terrorist organization was "an inappropriate choice of words" but then referred to the NEA's lobbying efforts as "obstructionist scare tactics…against Bush's historic education reforms".

The sting of his words remains, however, as Bush's war mentality touches all aspects of American life. A terrorist is a terrorist, and an idle accusation of such carries serious implications if you are not part of this right wing, big business administration.

While it is true that the NEA and the smaller union, American Federation of Teachers, initially supported NCLB, because it was a bipartisan plan that mandated regular testing of elementary and secondary school students. The hook was a threat of financial losses and possible school closures if the students failed to meet federal standards.

Both teachers' unions eventually opposed the program, when they determined that those federal standards targeted thousands of public schools for closure, forcing students into private schools. The unions accused Bush of backing out of his promises to provide enough funding to meet the mandated goals of the local school districts.

NCLB currently faces stiff opposition by educators, who testify that the federal standards are arbitrary and impossible to meet with resources that they have available in their school systems.

In a major concession by the Bush II Administration, Paige relaxed testing requirements, because schools with large numbers of immigrant students were unable to meet the English proficiency standards.

ROBERT ZOELLICK

A US Trade Representative, a Cabinet-level position, Robert Zoellick is one of the hawkish pro-Israel members of the Bush II Administration. His post carries the rank of Ambassador, and he is Bush II's chief trade policy advisor and trade negotiator.

Outside of his area of expertise, he consistently advocated invading Iraq and setting up a puppet government. You mean, like the one we have here?

One of fraudulent Enron's most influential paid consultants, Zoellick set out with ambitious plans to expand NAFTA (currently involving Canada, the US and Mexico) to include the rest of Latin America, plans strongly supported by US industry.

In his present position, Zoellick oversees the creation and implementation of policies promoting world growth. He directed China and Taiwan into the World Trade organization, influenced congressional action on the Jordan and Vietnam Trade Agreements, and worked with Congress to secure the Trade Act of 2002.

Critics blast Zoellick for talking out of both sides of his mouth. On one side, he talks about free trade, yet his ties to multinational corporations tell a different story. He serves Bush II well by confusing free trade as helping the American people while it really serves the interests of Bush's corporate cronies. In short, big business comes first.

Zoellick is the US free trade negotiator for the FTAA Pact, which would establish an agreement between 34 countries in the Western Hemisphere, except Cuba. None other than Jeb Bush lobbies hard for the FTAA headquarters to be established in Miami, and Katherine Harris — of hanging chad fame in the 2000 presidential election — considered the "godmother" of the FTAA — is involved in Jeb's efforts.

In 2003, Zoellick used the power of his office to suspend moves toward free trade talks with Egypt in retaliation for Egypt's refusal to back the US against Europe on the issue of genetically modified foods.

With scientific evidence to the contrary, Zoellick maintains his position on biotechnology. "In places where food is scarce or climates can be harsh, increased agricultural productivity through biotechnology can spell the difference between life and death, between health and disease, for millions of the world's poorest people."

That sounds good, but bottom line, it is all about the huge stakes at risk for corporate giants like Monsanto, DuPont, Dow and others that place policies ahead of people.

THE SUPREMES FIVE

If the five Supreme Court Justices had voted to sleep in on Saturday, December 12, 2000, George W. Bush might not have become President, and we would not be writing this book. Instead, they donned their robes and dubbed George W. Bush the 43rd President of the United States.

We cannot lay all the blame at the feet of five Supreme Court Justices, however. We would not be writing this book if Jeb Bush and Katherine Harris, Florida's former Secretary of State, had not deliberately disenfranchised black voters in the 2000 presidential election or if the final tally came down in any other state but Florida. Albert Gore — who won the national popular vote — would have been president.

The voting fiasco in Florida threw the decision into Bush-friendly hands in the United States Supreme Court. Those who voted for Bush II — and whom we can thank for giving us an inept president — the American Ali Baba and his 40 thieves — were: Chief Justice William Rehnquist, elevated to the top spot by Reagan, Chief Justice Antonio Scalia, a Reagan appointee, Chief Justice Anthony M. Kennedy, appointed by Reagan, Chief Justice Sandra Day O'Connor, a Reagan appointee, and Chief Justice Clarence Thomas, a Bush I nominee.

Runners-up

*Corporations have taken over the government
and turned it against its own people.*

Ralph Nader

ANDREW H. CARD, JR.

George W. Bush named Andrew Card his Chief of Staff to show his appreciation for his impressive service record in the two previous administrations. Card served as the US Secretary of Transportation under Bush I, as well as Assistant to the President and Deputy Chief of Staff.

In the private sector, Card served as Vice President of Government Relations at General Motors from 1999-2000, and as President/CEO of the American Automobile Manufacturers Association (AAMA) from 1993-98.

Perhaps we will best remember Andrew Card as the one who whispered into George W's ear that a plane hit Tower 2 of the World Trade Center on 9/11. Card immediately left the room, as if he knew in advance that Bush would not offer any comment or reaction. Bush continued reading about goats to elementary school children for several minutes until someone entered the room and told him to leave.

In *The New York Times* on September 7, 2002 Andrew Card echoed Karl Rove's thoughts on the launch of the war against Iraq, "From a marketing point of view, you don't introduce new products." He meant that you must take care — politically — when you launch a war.

Politics was very much a part of the White House decision to wage war. Card and Rove proved highly influential in furthering that agenda. They needed regime change in Iraq to influence the outcome of the 2002 elections and to divert public attention away from growing problems in the Bush II White House.

There was no shortage of problems; from Bush and Cheney's ties to Enron chief Ken Lay to the growing budget deficit to tax cuts for the rich, Ashcroft's excision of civil liberties, Bush's abandonment of vital international treaties, and the ongoing threat of al-Qaeda.

ELIOT A. COHEN

A noted scholar of military affairs at the Johns Hopkins School of Advanced International Studies (SAIS), like Wolfowitz before him, Eliot Cohen serves as Professor and Director of the Strategic Studies Program at SAIS.

He is one of the most influential neocons in the academic world. The neocon influence in academia raises concerns that today's young minds receive indoctrination into authoritarianism, military repression and neocon Islamophobia, all under the guise of counter-terrorism political studies.

Cohen currently serves on the Defense Policy Board, the think tank at the Pentagon severely criticized for conflicts of interest among its members, as well as their rigid ideology. Almost a third of the members come from the ultra-conservative Hoover Institution.

Cohen gained most notoriety for his premise that the War on Terrorism is really World War IV and the Cold War was World War III.

His affiliations include such hawkish advocacy groups as The Committee for the Liberation of Iraq and PNAC.

Cohen was one of several who signed the April 3, 2002 letter to Bush calling for removing Saddam Hussein from power and increasing support of Israel's war on terrorism.

TOM DELAY

United States House Majority Leader, Tom DeLay, a conservative Texas Republican, is an extreme right-wink Likudnik, who shares the philosophy of former US Senate Majority Leader, Richard Armey, also of Texas. Armey — and DeLay — support ethnic cleansing of Palestinians, forcibly removing all of them to neighboring Arab countries. This act, if not the suggestion, is an international war crime. Both DeLay, nicknamed "The Hammer" and Armey are openly bigoted and racist.

Considered one of the most powerful leaders ever to serve in Congress, DeLay has become the connection between corporation funding and politics in the nation's capitol. Ironically, a criminal investigation in Texas is underway regarding the illegal use of corporate donations by DELAY, INC. to get candidates elected to state offices. The charge is a violation of the Texas Election Code.

Like the majority of his fellow congressmen, DeLay receives financial benefits from supporting Israel. He has received $58,000 from AIPAC, the Israeli lobby. In a speech made before AIPAC, DeLay stated that the war in Iraq and Israel's battles against Palestinian terrorists are one in the same conflict. "We will win it," he asserted. "The survival of Israel is essential to America's victory in the war on terrorism, and America's victory in the war on terrorism is essential to Israel's survival. We will never leave their side."

DeLay received a standing ovation from AIPAC members when he called Bush II *the greatest friend of Israel in the world today. It was President Bush who realized Yasser Arafat had no intention of seeking peace, and therefore cut him off from any further negotiations, isolating him as the terrorist he is. It was President Bush who understood that the war America was waging against terrorism was the same war Israel had been fighting for decades.*

ARI FLEISCHER

Until 2003, Ari Fleischer served as the official White House spokesman under Bush II, propagating the lies and deception leading up to the Iraq War. A prominent member of the Jewish community, he most likely holds Israeli citizenship.

Fleischer has close ties to the Chabad Lubavitch Hasidics, a pro-Israeli extremist group that follows Qabala and holds very insulting views of even Jews, who do not embrace their extremist views. He is the former co-president of Chabad's Capitol Jewish Forum.

ROBERT KAGAN

A co-founder of PNAC, Robert Kagan is Senior Associate at the Carnegie Endowment for International Peace and contributing editor of *The Weekly Standard*. He served as Deputy for Policy in the Reagan State Department. His father, Donald, a Yale historian, was a liberal Democrat who switched to a neocon in the 1970s. Donald and Frederick, Robert's brother, published *While America Sleeps*, which called for increased defense spending. All three Kagans, since then, have warned repeatedly that even the rapidly growing Pentagon budget is insufficient for conquering the world.

CHARLES KRAUTHAMMER

A neocon intellectual, Jewish-American journalist and staunch Israeli supporter, Charles Krauthammer pushed Bush II for regime change in Iraq as a prelude to furthering the neocon drive for New World Order. Soon after 9/11, Krauthammer focused on Baghdad as the first war target.

For him, the war in Iraq was about three things: (1) removing Saddam's weapons of mass destruction, (2) canceling the deal that said as long as they sent oil, we would not interfere in their internal affairs, and (3) rebuilding the Arab World.

According to Krauthammer, the US had no choice but to launch a preemptive war. *In the 21st Century, we face a new and singular challenge: the democratization of mass destruction. Three possible strategies lie in the face of that challenge: appeasement, deterrence and preemption. Because appeasement and deterrence will not work, preemption is the only strategy left.*

Despite all the difficulties and scandals that indicate failure of great magnitude there, he remains convinced that the US will ultimately emerge victorious. True to the neocon creed, the US must win.

KENNETH LAY

The former CEO of Enron, Kenneth Lay has skated on all charges for the scandalous demise of his corporation that ruined the lives of thousands of people. Protection comes to those who contribute handsomely to George W's campaigns for Governor of Texas and President of the United States. As we have said before, it pays to have friends in high places.

The Enron scandal grew enormously when tapes, replete with profanity, revealed Enron employees celebrating California's last energy crisis brought on by creating shortages to drive electricity prices up. Employees cheered over the devastating wildfires and thoughts of stealing from grandmothers.

EDWARD LUTTWAK

Supposedly an Israeli citizen, who has taught in Israel, Edward Luttwak serves as a member of the National Security Study Group of the Department of Defense at the Pentagon. The main theme in many of his articles expresses his extremism toward Israel in calling for the US war against Iraq.

WALDEN O'DELL

The CEO of the Ohio-based Diebold company, which makes the controversial electronic voting machines that leave no paper trails, Walden O'Dell is an extremely partisan Republican who vowed that Bush II would win the 2004 presidential election. He donated generously to the GOP in 2000. O'Dell became CEO of Diebold following the mysterious death in May 2003 of former CEO Wesley Vance.

Voter fraud and incorrect totals with paperless electronic voting machines continues to stir debate around the country and drive some states to adopt the use of machines that provide a paper trail. One example of the kind of problem that results with paperless machines occurred in Indiana, where some precincts ran out of Republican ballots shortly after the polls opened. Some counties there reported thousands more votes than registered voters. Voters, beware!

MICHAEL POWELL

The son of Colin Powell, Secretary of State, learned early in the Bush II Administration that nepotism is a good thing. Bush II appointed Powell as chairman of the Federal Communications Commission (FCC), giving him untold latitude in manipulating the US media and the information that the public receives.

OTTO REICH

Bush II appointed Otto Reich to serve as Assistant Secretary of State for Western Hemisphere, a top job for Latin America. One wonders what criteria Bush used to make this appointment, considering Reich's complicity in the Salvadoran bloodbath, and the deception of the Congress and American people that followed.

That is not his only claim to notoriety. He was the Director of the now-defunct Office of Public Diplomacy (OPD), which the House Committee on Foreign Affairs censured in 1987 for "prohibited covert propaganda activities", according to *The Washington Post*.

ROBERT SATLOFF

Another pro-Israel hawk in a long list of them in the Bush II Administration, Robert Satloff serves as the US National Security Council Advisor. He is a former Executive Director of the Washington Institute for Near East Policy (WINEAP), which is the think tank of the Israeli lobby, AIPAC. He currently serves as the Institute's Director of Policy and Strategic Planning.

An expert on Arab and Islamic politics, Satloff ran into serious opposition when Bush II considered him for Special Assistant to the President and Senior Director of the Near East and South Asia Office of the National Security Office.

The primary reason for opposition was that WINEAP essentially is an extension of AIPAC, the Israeli lobby. Executive Director, Satloff was one of Israel's foremost advocates in the United States. The connection seems to be inappropriate, at least.

GEORGE TENET

I never would have agreed to the formulation of the Central Intelligence Agency (CIA) back in 1947 if I had known it would become the American Gestapo. – Harry S. Truman

According to John Stockwell, former CIA official, *The CIA has been running thousands of operations over the years. There have been about 3,000 major covert operations and over 10,000 minor covert operations, all designed*

95

to disrupt, destabilize or modify the activities of other countries. But they are all illegal. They raise serious questions about the moral responsibility of the United States in the international society of nations.

George Tenet, CIA Director under Bush II, continued his position from the Clinton presidency. The CIA conducts intelligence gathering around the world, and during the wars in Afghanistan and Iraq has played a major role in delivering intelligence to the Pentagon. Rumsfeld and Tenet are not friends; in fact, there is considerable tension between them, because Rumsfeld prefers to use military intelligence than involve the CIA.

When the Abu Ghraib prisoner abuse scandals surfaced, all the principle players of the Bush II Administration pointed fingers rather than accept moral responsibility for the crimes committed in Iraq. The CIA is just one of them.

Bush II recently fired Tenet over an apparent disloyalty issue but allowed him to designate his departure a resignation. Many speculated that Rumsfeld would leave office, but it seems that Tenet became the fall guy.

A final note from John Stockwell: *It is the functioning of the CIA to keep the world unstable and to propagandize and teach the American people to hate, so we will let the Establishment spend any amount of money on arms.*

DOV ZAKHEIM

According to some estimates, we cannot track $2.3 trillion in transactions.
Donald Rumsfeld, CBS News, January 29, 2002
[2.3 trillion is the equivalent of $8,000 for every American.]

Dov Zakheim resigned in 2004 as the Undersecretary of Defense (Comptroller) and Chief Financial Officer (CFO) at the Pentagon. At least partly on his watch, the Pentagon came up short $2.3 trillion.

Zakheim, an ordained rabbi who holds Israeli citizenship, works closely with AIPAC, the Israeli lobby. He was Bush II's Jewish foreign policy advisor.

If you think you read this profile incorrectly, let us repeat. An Israeli citizen and ordained rabbi was the Chief Financial officer of the United States Department of Defense, which is missing $2.3 trillion.

In his farewell comments, Zakheim said, "We are in the business of fighting wars. We are not in the business of balancing books." [No fooling, Dov.] "We have made great strides in rectifying the department's antiquated financial management system. We continue to anticipate that defense will receive clean audits in the not too distant future." After they find the missing $2.3 trillion.

Truth Thieves -
The Mainstream Media

The great masses of people will more easily fall victims to a big lie than a small one, especially if it is repeated over and over.

Adolph Hitler

It would satisfy their egos too much to give any of the Truth Thieves a substantial amount of space or position in this book, so they appear toward the end with minimal credit for their thieving ways.

The bottom line is that in their zeal, based on right-wing ideology, religion or sheer lunacy, they collectively stole the public's right to know the truth. As direct White House pipelines, fed the approved Ashcroft lingo of the day, the mainstream media have broken the rules of true journalism. They have not ferreted out the truth, raised important questions, or challenged this Administration. Instead of reporting from the battlefield as their predecessors did in World Wars I and II, they succumbed to being embedded with the military in Iraq, gobbling up only one side of the story and spewing it out over the airwaves to the American sheeple.

There is no way that the mainstream media, with millions of dollars in cash flow and staffs in the thousands, missed the signs of deception that were so obvious to bloggers running web sites on spare change. The lies and deception fed the American people by the mainstream media were intentional. They are complicit in this Administration's war crimes.

More than denying the American public their right to the truth about what is really happening in this country, some of the more notable talk show hosts stoop to the lowest levels of hate mongering. They applaud torture and humiliation of prisoners, believing that these subhuman enemies deserve what they get. In typical wartime propaganda, they seek creative ways to dehumanize the enemy, making it easier to stir up hatred in their listeners. They make the unthinkable patriotic!

RUPERT MURDOCH

Australian media entrepreneur and managing director of News Corp, Rupert Murdoch has emerged as the only media executive in the United States that owns all three broadcast assets: broadcast, cable and satellite channels. The latter came in December 2003 with his $6.6 take-over of GM's DirecTV, approved by the FCC (remember, Michael Powell is at the helm there). In short, Murdoch went global, and in a big way, with his latest buyout that added 11 million subscribers to his audience.

In addition to DirecTV, Murdoch owns FOX broadcast network, FOX cable news, 20th Century Fox, 35 US television stations, the *New York Post,* the *Times* and *Sun* newspapers (both in London). He also owns *The Weekly Standard*, HarperCollins Publishing, and the National Geographic cable channel. News Corp's revenues in 2002 were $17 billion. With DirecTV, his revenues have skyrocketed.

Murdoch, more than any other media mogul, influences his audiences with blatant pro-Bush II Administration propaganda. Support of the Iraq War and other Bush II programs provide Murdoch's news outlets with ample fodder to feed to the American sheeple.

In a recent "20/20" exposé, Murdoch's DirecTV rakes in more than $500 million in unreported revenue from its soft- and hard-core pornography made available to home viewers for a premium. All in a day's work.

RUSH LIMBAUGH

This pill-popping, hypocritical giant of the airwaves needs no introduction. He reigns as king of radio-sponsored hate mongering that no person of intelligence can tolerate hearing. He incites public support for an illegal war, spews venom at the enemy du jour, and applauds despicable treatment of prisoners in violation of all international human rights laws. His hour-long highly partisan talk show enjoys exclusive access to US troops in Iraq as the only program broadcast daily over American Forces Radio.

BILL O'REILLY, SEAN HANNITY, MICHAEL SAVAGE

Since there are just so many ways to define hate mongering, and they have already been used to describe the broadcasts of Rush Limbaugh, we are lumping these three cable TV blabbermouths into one section. If these clowns would shut up, stop interrupting, and let their guests speak on the subject, about which they are qualified to speak, maybe they would learn something. Apparently, it is easier for them to serve as White House mouthpieces instead of thinking for themselves. It is difficult to imagine anyone in their positions not questioning the events and activities of the Bush II Administration.

NETWORK & CABLE NEWS

Whatever happened to journalists, who prided themselves on seeking and finding the truth about any story? During the Bush II Administration, those journalists have become mere reporters, giving the American people what the Administration wants them to know, not allowing them to know the truth. A deliberate cover up of the truth leaves the public in the dark, making it easier for the Administration to manipulate the masses and move closer to the absolute control of a police or military state.

NEWSPAPERS

Newspapers are unable, seemingly, to discriminate between a bicycle accident and the collapse of a civilization.
George Bernard Shaw

The New York Times, The Washington Post, and virtually all other notable newspapers throughout the country followed the lead of the Bush II Administration in funneling lies and deception instead of bucking the system and telling the truth. Their complicity in the Administration's war crimes is noted. Long after alternative sources on the Internet reported the truth, the mainstream papers started to play catch up. Too late.

The rare exceptions to mainstream media sources delivering the truth to the American people appear in the next section.

Points of Light Awards

*It is the duty of the patriot to protect
his country from its government.*

Thomas Paine

There you have it. The American Ali Baba and his 40 Thieves. Together, they are complicit of stealing America's best and brightest, sending them off to an illegal war. Their costly agendas, created in the dark shadows around George Bush II, amass fortunes for them and their corporate cohorts.

Now that we have told the dark and sordid story, we would like to offer hope to the reader. To do so, we give Points of Light Awards to a number of daring and deserving Americans. George Herbert Walker Bush (Bush I) initiated the idea of Points of Light awards, suggesting that Americans across the country who shed their light through their good deeds should be recognized.

Since Bush II and his 40 neocon thieves, runners-up or mainstream media thieves have not earned Points of Light Awards, we give them to the following:

MIKE RIVERO — whatreallyhappened.com, for providing the best alternative source of news on the Internet and for serving on the front lines of true journalism, dissecting deception and unraveling lies. For the past 10 years, Rivero has been true to his motto, "There are two sides to every question, and then there is what really happened." His anti-war, anti-lie web site shows no political party favorites, but calls lies as he sees them, and challenges people to think beyond what the mainstream media spews.

Once a government resorts to terror against its own population to get what it wants, it must keep using terror against its own population to get what it wants. A government that terrorizes its own people can never stop. If such a government ever lets the fear subside and rational thought return to the populace, that government is finished.

SEYMOUR HERSCH — *The New Yorker*, for demonstrating the grit, fortitude and moral fiber of a true journalist, for exposing the scandal of Iraqi prisoner abuse, just as he exposed the My Lai massacre in the Viet Nam war.

CHRIS MATTHEWS — CNBC "Hardball" host, for breaking away from the pack of Bush brown-nosers and opposing the Oil War II, when his embedded peers in Iraq were listening only to the beat of the Bush drums and repeating the lies and deception of this Administration.

CBS "60 MINUTES" — for courageously airing the first network television coverage of prisoner abuse at Abu Ghraib Prison in Iraq.

HELEN THOMAS — for telling it like it is in Washington, from a position of true knowledge. The feisty first lady of White House press conferences, who no longer sits in the front row and asks the first question of the President, served seven presidents. She confesses that Bush II is the worst president in American history.

MICHAEL MOORE — for his gutsy presentations on film that make people think — most recently "Fahrenheit 911", which links the Bushes and bin Ladens and exposes the ill-conceived Iraq War launched by Bush II and his neocon thieves.

GENERAL ANTHONY ZINNI — for not only having the foresight to see that the plan for Iraq War II was poorly planned, but also for daring to speak out against the flawed strategy from the beginning.

> *All those that believed this [war] was going to be the catalyst for some kind of positive change...didn't understand the region, the culture, the situation and the issues. We had to create a false rationale for going in to get public support. The rationale that we faced an imminent threat, or a serious threat, was ridiculous.*

Zinni knows. He served as chief of the US Central Command, the same post held by General Tommy Franks in the Iraq War and by General Norman Schwarzkopf in Desert Storm.

> *It's pretty interesting that all the generals see it the same way, and all the others who have never fired a shot, and are hot to go to war, see it another...We are about to do something that will ignite a fuse in this region that we will rue the day we ever started.*

RICHARD CLARKE — for speaking the truth about the Iraq War in his book *Against All Enemies*, in which he clearly reveals that Saddam Hussein posed no threat to the United States, that Iraq had no weapons of mass destruction, and that the pre-emptive war was therefore illegal. In his book, he states that there had not been any evidence or intelligence (CIA or Mossad) of any terrorism plots against the United States from 1993 to 2003.

SCOTT RITTER — for publicly insisting from the beginning that Iraq had no weapons of mass destruction. As a former UN weapons inspector in Iraq, he knew what he was talking about, and he never wavered. Talk about vindication! In mid-June 2004, the American public finally believes that the War in Iraq was unfounded. Way to go, Scott!

SENATOR ERNEST HOLLINGS (SC) — for being one of a handful of US Congress critters and Senators, who dare to speak the truth that Israel controls the US government and exercises pervasive powers in virtually all walks of life in America. "Of course, there were no weapons of mass destruction," he wrote in an article published in the *Charleston Post and Courier* on May 6, 2004. *Israel's intelligence, Mossad, knows what's going on in Iraq. They are the best. They have to know. Israel's survival depends on knowing. Israel long since would have taken us to the weapons of mass destruction if there were any or if they had been removed. With Iraq no threat, why invade a sovereign country? The answer: President Bush's policy to secure Israel.*

SENATOR ROBERT BYRD (WV) — for his steadfast, relentless voice against giving war powers to the President, arguing that such power belongs only to the Congress. When his attempt to stage a filibuster against the Iraq War Resolution was defeated, he continued to argue against giving a blank check to Bush II, saying it was "the Tonkin Gulf resolution all over again. Let us stop, look and listen. Let us not give this President or any President unchecked power. Remember the Constitution."

RAMSEY CLARK — former US Attorney General, for leading the call to impeach President George W. Bush (www.votetoimpeach.org), drafting 17 Articles of Impeachment, and for his courageous activism toward the preservation of peace, justice and humanitarianism. Clark's service to America and the world is virtually unparalleled.

The United States is not nearly so concerned that its acts be kept secret from its intended victims as it is that the American people not know them.

CONGRESSWOMAN SHEILA JACKSON-LEE (TX) — for standing tall against Bush's pre-emptive war in Iraq, and for continuing to speak out for the rights of all Americans. After Congress and the Senate approved the Iraq War Resolution, Congresswoman Jackson-Lee introduced House Concurrent Resolution 102, which states that only Congress has "the sole and exclusive power to declare war." Congressman John Conyers (MI) was the only co-sponsor of HR 102.

CONGRESSMAN DENNIS KUCINICH (OH) — for his consistent opposition to the war. After the Congress and Senate approved the Iraq War Resolution, Congressman Kucinich introduced House Concurrent Resolution 101. It expressed that Public Law 107-243, authorizing Bush II to use military force against Saddam Hussein, was "null and void." He had no co-sponsors on that resolution. Kucinich waged a robust presidential campaign that challenged Americans to take back the power that their forefathers gave to them more than 200 years ago.

RALPH NADER — for courageously standing for truth and fairness in consumer issues, political campaigns, and international policy, for consistently presenting the best alternative to the two-party system, and for continuously inspiring citizens to participate in building a more democratic world.

LYNDON LaROUCHE — for representing the "forgotten man" who faces ruin in the ongoing Global Depression and neocon drive for perpetual war, for his astute analysis of world events, global economy and American crises. *America's Number One problem is that it does not know itself.*

Posthumously to

Former **SENATOR PAUL WELLSTONE** — whose light for truth, justice and peace, tragically extinguished, shines on, giving hope that one day truth and justice will reign, and there will be peace for all peoples of the earth.

Finally, to the **HUNDREDS OF MILLIONS OF PEOPLE** the world over — for protesting an illegal war and for demonstrating global solidarity in the name of peace.

*This country, with its institutions, belongs to the people who inhabit it.
Whenever they shall grow weary of the existing government,
they can exercise their constitutional right of amending it or
exercise their revolutionary right to overthrow it.*

Abraham Lincoln

*History will have to record that the greatest tragedy of this period was
not the strident clamor of bad people but the
appalling silence of good people.*

Dr. Martin Luther King, Jr.

About the Author

Born in Lebanon in 1946, Alex Shami became an orphan at the age of four. A year later, former Lebanese President Shamoun and his wife, Zalfa, the First Lady of Lebanon, adopted him. Alex served with the Lebanese Police Force, Squad 16, beginning in 1964. After immigrating to the United States in 1975, he launched a Lebanese & Middle East live television program on Detroit's Channel 62. He served the US Army for four years.

Professor Shami holds nine undergraduate and graduate degrees. He has taught in Detroit public schools and community colleges since 1991. He won elections to six-year terms on the Dearborn School Board and Henry Ford Community College Board. Currently serving as a Full Professor of English and Psychology at Wayne County Community College Detroit, Dr. Shami chairs the ESL Department.

Professor Shami and his wife, Iman, live in Dearborn, Michigan.

www.ingramcontent.com/pod-product-compliance
Lightning Source LLC
Chambersburg PA
CBHW051450280526
45785CB00003B/1501